OPEN THIS LETTER IN TEN YEARS

Life Lessons
from
Dad's Love Letters

Linda DeHoff
and
Bill Butterworth

Published by Linda DeHoff

ISBN 978-1-387-72789-6

Dedication

My precious Bill, Joe, Jackie, Miles, Drew and Claire,

I wrote this story for you upon being inspired by a dear friend that demanded my story be told. The letters from your great grandfather to your great grandmother, the love of his life, and to me, his six-year-old daughter, are a tale of love; love for a daughter he believes he may not see again, because he knows only the hell, fear and loneliness of war and being unable to share his hopes and dreams for his only child. You may find the concepts of love, faith, and devotion to family a bit outdated, but I encourage you to look deeply at these lessons that they may someday become your truth.

Your loving grandmother,

Nana

Acknowledgments

I offer deep appreciation and gratitude to David Baker, President of the Pro Football Hall of Fame, who encouraged me to share these personal letters and for introducing me to the sensitive and talented author, Bill Butterworth.

I am indebted to my husband Bob for his encouragement, guidance and love throughout our life together.

I remain proud of and grateful to our children Molly and Daniel for their example of leadership, patience and sense of humor; but most of all, for their love for one another and family.

I sincerely thank the team of Jim Porter, Julie Tyrrell and Casey Richards for their patience and contributions.

Last, but not least, my parents, who by example, provided me with love, abundance and faith throughout my life. I am eternally grateful.

TABLE OF CONTENTS

Introduction

A Letter to the Reader

Dear Precious Reader,

Since I formatted this book around a series of letters, I thought it helpful to write a letter to you so that you will have a better understanding of how this book came into being and what I hope to accomplish with its writing.

In October of 2019, my husband Bob and I invited some dear friends over for dinner to our home, just outside of Canton, Ohio. David and Colleen Baker are a delightful couple. Colleen and I get along perfectly, and David raves about my Italian cooking.

According to David, the main course was another Sicilian triumph as we cleared the table for dessert and coffee. In the steady stream of conversation, we navigated through a variety of topics before turning to memories of our parents, which have always been a favorite subject of mine. As we focused in on our fathers in particular, I made mention of a detail that many find interesting. "My dad was in the Army during World War II and then again in Korea," I began. "He wrote home to

Mom and me all the time." The Baker's eyes widened when I added, "And I still have the letters that he wrote us."

That led to me bringing out a handful of the letters written by my father. I had never brought out these letters to anyone other than our family and I was intrigued by how fascinated the Bakers were in seeing them. David seemed especially absorbed. I guess that makes sense. David is the President of the Pro Football Hall of Fame in town, so a large part of his world includes being surrounded by memorabilia from the past. He seemed as captivated by my father's letters as he would have been with Vince Lombardi's playbook or Jim Thorpe's contract.

As I handed him a few of Dad's letters, I came upon my favorite, which I handed to David with great care. "This is a letter that my dad wrote to me during the Korean War when I was six years old," I said, as David nodded and gently took it into his large hands. "What makes it so interesting to me is that he didn't want me to open the letter until I was sixteen…" David looked up from the letter with a quizzical expression, unsure if he heard me correctly.

"It's a letter mostly about love and marriage," I explained. "I think Dad wrote it to me back then, just in case he wouldn't return home."

David read the letter through completely—it's ten pages of beautiful cursive longhand—and then lovingly placed it back down on the table.

David Baker is a big man, physically. Like NFL offensive lineman big. To see him handle that letter so carefully and then see him with tears in his eyes as he finished it was truly a juxtaposition. "This is beautiful," the gentle giant said softly.

"My dad was a very special man," I replied.

After a moment or two of silence, David said, "You should put these letters in a book." I smiled and nodded but didn't really take him seriously.

"People would be inspired by your Dad's love for you," David continued. It quickly became apparent that David wasn't kidding. "You need to share these letters with the whole world."

"That's a really good idea," Bob encouraged.

Before I knew it, I was joining in the conversation. "Can you imagine a parent writing a letter like that to every newborn?" I suggested.

"Make it available in every hospital birthing area," Colleen suggested.

"Dad loved Mom and me. He lived life as a mission. He had morals. He was upright. He was a good soldier. He cared about others. He lived the life God wanted him to live," I said.

"This book could be a sort of prescription for a good life," David added. "As well as a perfect gift for a soldier, a veteran or any mom or dad."

I nodded.

"I think you should seriously consider it," David pressed. "Colleen and I would be more than happy to help you in any way we can in order for you to make it happen."

I nodded again, my mind racing.

Then David added another comment, laden with meaning and significance. "I don't think it's an accident that we all met together here tonight."

*   *   *

And that was the birth of what you hold in your hands today. I've read over my father's letters and have carefully chosen a dozen or so to include for you to read. Stylistically, I've mixed it up—some letters will make you laugh, some will make you cry. There are chapters that will be followed by some explanation, while others will stand on their own. And throughout the book, I will season the entrees with some background material in order for you to better appreciate my dad.

You'll smile when you read the parts of the letters that clearly illustrate the fact that he was writing in the 1940s and 1950s. Some things have changed. Some for the better, but some not so much. At least that's how I see it.

I've attempted to include letters that will provide some practical take-away applications to your life, without becoming preachy. However, Dad was a man of strong conviction, so be forewarned.

The book is thematic, not chronological. In no particular order we'll start on Pearl Harbor and before the book is finished, we will travel to Japan, Sicily, New York City, San Francisco, Washington D.C. and of course, our wonderful hometown of Canton, Ohio.

One part missing from the equation is not being able to read all of these letters as they were originally penned with my father's impeccable handwriting. Some of the letters seem to magically move from cursive to calligraphy. It definitely added to the charm.

By the time we're finished together, you will love my dad. If you don't, I have somehow failed in my job as his conduit.

So, I invite you now to enter a world that at first blush will appear to be from a fairy tale, but my hope is that you will be inspired to make that world a place of your own in our 21st century.

Love,

Linda DeHoff

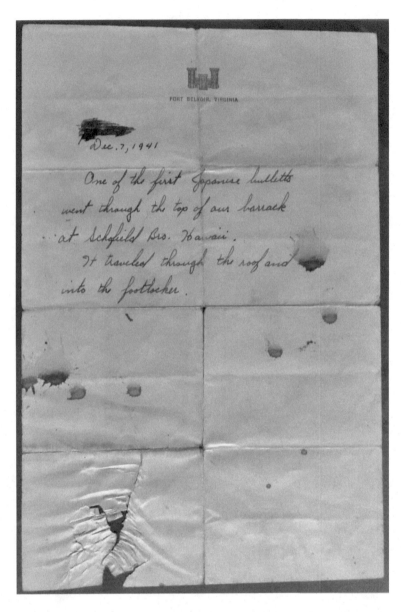

FORT BELVOIR, VIRGINIA

Dec. 7, 1941

One of the first Japanese bulletts
went through the top of our barrack
at Schfield Bro. Hawaii.
It traveled through the roof and
into the footlocker.

Dec 7, 1941, Pearl Harbor, bullet passed through stationary.

Chapter One
The Sergeant

His military ID card described him as 5 feet, 8 ½ inches tall, 170 pounds, brown eyes, black hair, and ruddy complexion. His grade was Sergeant. He was part of Company C, 34th Engineers. His serial number was 35026535. He was 24 years old, stationed at the Schofield Barracks on Pearl Harbor. It was 1941.

On December 7th of that year, the Japanese made a surprise attack on that very site. It began around 7:55 in the morning and came in two waves. The first wave of attack lasted approximately eleven minutes. The second wave arrived at 8:40 and the shocking surprise was over an hour later. The attack killed 2,403 service members and wounded 1,178 more. It sank or destroyed 6 U.S. ships, along with 169 planes.

Later in the day on that infamous Sunday, the young sergeant took a few minutes to send a short letter back home to his family. Looking at the letter in its present form, the sheet of stationery is far from perfect. Large stains dot the page, alongside rips in the paper itself in no particular pattern. However, the sergeant's beautiful handwriting stands in vivid contrast to the tattered page:

Dec. 7, 1941

One of the first Japanese bullets went through the top of our barrack at Schofield Brs. Hawaii.

It traveled through the roof and into the footlocker.

Back on the mainland, his parents, Michael and Theresa, were delighted to hear the good news that their son was still alive. The sergeant was part of a large family—eight children born to Michael and Theresa in nine quick years. Five of the offspring were sons and all five served in the military during the same painful stretch of years known as World War II.

Michael and Theresa were originally from Sicily, but early in their marriage the adventurous young immigrants made their way to a new life in the United States. Michael came over first and settled in the South

Market Italian neighborhood of Canton, Ohio. Theresa followed later, chaperoned by her brother. It was there the large family grew up. To this day that area of town still produces some of the most delicious Italian cuisine one could ever hope to enjoy.

Tucked away in a photo album is an 8x10, black and white family photo of the couple surrounded by seven of their children, all of which are young adults. They are a very handsome family indeed. At first glance the entire family could all be described the same way the sergeant was described on his Army ID card—brown eyes, black (wavy) hair and ruddy complexion—all of them with the exception of Theresa, who has light colored hair and fairer skin. A second glance highlights the varied height in the family. Michael, in true patriarchal form, towers over everyone, while Theresa, in the role of loving mama, looks strong, yet quite petite. Officially, Michael was 6'6" and Theresa was 4'9". (I find myself smiling, creating an imaginary scenario where the two of them met while both were members of the Italian Olympic team—Michael playing basketball and Theresa competing in gymnastics—that's not what happened, but it sounds fun). In the photo, Theresa stands next to her husband, the crown of her head barely reaching the height of his strong, broad shoulders.

One of the sons is almost as tall as Michael. Three other sons are another few inches shorter. The shortest of the five sons is son number three—the sergeant.

The occasion for the photo has long been forgotten, but it was a day to wear their Sunday best. The women are in lovely dresses with their hair perfectly arranged, while the men are all clad in suits. Just like their father, the sons wear neckties—all except one son, that is. The sergeant has chosen an open collar white shirt, its elongated collar stretching out over the wide lapels of his two-button suit.

The facial expressions in the photo are intriguing. Father and mother wear warm, sincere smiles on their faces. Not silly grins, but genuine expressions of joy. The two daughters have lovely smiles, too. The sergeant's four brothers run the gamut of expression: a full smile, just the hint of a smile, a more stoic look, as well as a legitimate look of sternness. It's the sergeant's face that captures one's attention. He is smiling freely, with his head cocked ever-so-slightly to his left. But it's his eyes that stand out and draw you in. His eyes are smiling. If a washcloth was placed over the lower part of his face, say from the nose down, one would still be convinced that the sergeant is smiling. One final overview of the family photo shows that the other four sons make up the back row of the family shot. Instead of all five boys standing in back, with the two girls surrounding their parents in the front row, one of the daughters is in the back, and right up front next to his 6'6" father is the sergeant. Most likely, he was in the front because he was the shortest of the boys.

Hmmm. But maybe not. Maybe there was more to being invited to stand next to his father than meets the eye.

Pictured: The Sturrett Family, back row (left to right): Carl, Johnny, Angie, Joe, Angelo; front row (left to right): Tony, Michael, Theresa, Connie.

*　　*　　*

A few years after that family photo, the sergeant would find himself on Pearl Harbor. It was an advantageous assignment for him.

11

Since golf courses are open year-round in Hawaii, he could pursue his passionate love of the sport. In his wallet, he carried his membership card to the Schofield Golf Association:

This is to certify that Anton M. Sturrett is a member in good standing of the Schofield Golf Association and is entitled to play on the course for the month of December, 1941.

That was the sergeant's name. Anton Sturrett.

Better known as Tony.

Better known to me as Dad.

Chapter Two

Love Is Like A Lovely Flower

Dad was a good soldier.

He rose to the rank of Captain, working tirelessly in the Army Corps of Engineers. We will uncover more on my father's military career in future chapters.

After World War II, Tony was back home in Ohio for a while, but not for long. Soon he was called back into service with the Corps of Engineers, but this time in the Korean conflict. It's these military experiences that helped shape who he was and how he chose to live his life.

But there is another key character in this story. Tony's wife, Helen. My mom. To say my father loved my mother deeply is like saying springtime can be kind of pretty. He adored her.

During their years of geographic separation while he served in the Army, Dad was a faithful letter writer. He would write to Mom in abundance and he even wrote to me as his little girl.

Here's an example of a letter he wrote to my mother shortly after I was born:

My darling wife and daughter,

I miss you very much today, darling. Not that I don't always miss you, but today I'm a bit more than just lonely for you. I'm really hungry for you. I want you in my arms—kissing you—or even pushing in your nose. Gee I love you. I think we were meant for one another, and you've now become as important to me as water is to soup. Ha! Figure it out—that's pretty important.

I called you about 5:45 today but you were up at Nani's. Ange told me Linda weighed 4 lbs. 5 ½ ounces. Isn't that wonderful! At that rate she will soon weigh the necessary 5 pounds. Ha!

I asked Ange to have you call me after 9:00 tonight. I'll finish this letter after I talk to you.

Gee, it was swell talking to you tonight. I can hardly wait till you come back. I want so much to have you and our "little one" near me.

Perhaps you've noticed a difference in me since Linda has arrived, but darling I feel more. I've always loved you this way darling. Perhaps I show it more now than I did before Linda was born, but I don't know how I could love you more. Linda or 10 children couldn't make me love you more darling—that's impossible, because I love you as much as can be loved right now. As long as we love the way we do darling we will go through life happy. We must never give one another reason to doubt or distrust. Love is like a lovely flower. You can look at it—smell it—adore it, but never abuse it or it will die. I'm sure we will never abuse ours because our love got all its abuse the first two months of our marriage. Our flower has weathered the storm and spring frosts—it has blossomed into a beautiful flower with a little bud (Linda) for all to take notice of. When I'm with you I'm as happy as I can possibly be.

I must close now darling. I hope you don't think I've gone mushy, because I haven't. I'm still as rough as ever, and I'd probably be pushing your nose—biting or twisting your arm around a bedpost—or even smashing your finger in a nutcracker if you were here right now. Ha! I guess I feel a little sentimental today.

Good night darling—may God bless you always (Linda too)

Your loving husband,

Pop

X x

P.S. I'll even take Linda for a walk once in awhile.

P.S: When she learns how to change her own diaper. Ha!

Gee, I love you Momie

Pictured: Helen and Tony.

Tony Sturrett and Helen Berry made a beautiful couple. Just like Tony, Helen had seven siblings in her family. They married on April 8, 1944. I came along a year later, born prematurely, a mere 3 pounds.

She was as Scotch Irish as he was Sicilian Italian. My mom was faithful, hardworking and unselfish, yet with a fun-loving spirit as counterpoint. She was quite the artist and possessed a lovely singing voice. At one point in her life, she sang with a big band. I can just imagine her on the bandstand, dressed to the nines in a long flowing gown, her hair carefully combed in the style of the day. The saxes, trombones and trumpets belt out the intro as she confidently walks forward to the large silver microphone. All eyes are on her as she flawlessly delivers the lyrics to the latest tune by Glenn Miller or Tommy Dorsey. What a pleasant sound!

She was a very attractive woman and could melt steel with her broad and beautiful smile. Tony and Helen were a striking couple. One of my favorite family photos shows Dad proudly holding me when I was around one year old. Mom is standing next to us, with her head thrown back, a smile having just exploded onto her pretty face. She was wonderful. Everyone, and I mean everyone, loved Mom.

Pictured: Helen, Linda, and Tony in Alexandria, VA.

Like I said, they made a wonderful couple. They never fought.

Well, actually that's not entirely true. There was one subject that would

cause dissension in the ranks...

...pasta.

Mom would lovingly cook a big bowl of pasta, serve it up and wait

for Dad to praise it, which was his normal routine when it came to Mom's

cooking of other dishes. But not with pasta.

"This is overcooked," Dad would announce, scrunching up his

face and pushing the plate away from his place at the table.

If that wasn't shocking enough, one time Mom grabbed the bowl

of pasta and hurled it onto the floor with a mighty crash.

18

"How do you like it now, Tony?" she responded, leaving Dad in charge of making his own dinner.

*   *   *

Excluding pasta preparation, I learned so much about how to have a happy marriage just by watching Mom and Dad together. As I reread Dad's letters to Mom during his Army years, I arrive at a deeper understanding of their love and happiness together, and what each meant to the other.

Love Has to be Expressed. It Shouldn't be Held in.

I miss you very much today, darling. Not that I don't always miss you, but today I'm a bit more than just lonely for you. I'm really hungry for you. I want you in my arms—kissing you—or even pushing in your nose. Gee I love you.

Especially back in the 1940s and 1950s, men were not encouraged to be in touch with their feelings. If they ever dared to express how they felt, it was usually followed by an apology. It was the era of the 'macho man' and women were expected to put up with it.

19

But Dad wasn't that way. Sure, he was a rough, tough soldier who could lead his troops into battle, but he also had a soft side to him. A loving side. A caring side. I have dozens of the letters that my dad wrote to my mom and there is a consistency throughout all of them—Dad did not hold back on how he felt about Mom.

Love in Marriage is Like What the Bible Says—Two Become One.

Gee I love you. I think we were meant for one another, and you've now become as important to me as water is to soup. Ha! Figure it out—that's pretty important.

I don't know if Dad realized what he was saying when he used the analogy of soup and water, but I do know that upon reflection, that is quite a profound statement. In the first book of the Bible, God explains what a marriage looks like in clear and simple terms:

This explains why a man leaves his father and mother and is joined to his wife, and the two are united into one.

—Genesis 2:24.

Two become one. Sure, they're still two individuals who do their own things and have separate gifts, talents and interests. (Dad has more to say about that in another letter we'll look at.) But there's the other aspect of the couple acting in perfect union. They're in sync, finishing one another's sentences. There's a comfort together. Safety. Trust.

Love is Not Automatic. It Takes Effort. But the Results are Rich.

As long as we love the way we do darling we will go through life happy.

Dad and Mom knew that love took work. They knew you don't wake up one morning and magically know all there is to know about love. No, it's not that simple. Instead, you wake up every morning and essentially make the decision that you're going to love that person in your life. Dad communicated his love for Mom constantly through his letters. There wasn't any "I told you 'I love you' in the last letter so I won't have to say it now." His expressions of love were consistent. They were on his lips till his dying day. *As long as we love the way we do darling we will go through life happy.* And they did.

To Dad, Love was Both Tough and Tender.

I hope you don't think I've gone mushy, because I haven't. I'm still as rough as ever

Can you imagine my dad writing a letter like this one in his Army barracks? There's not a great deal of privacy in those quarters. I'm wondering if a fellow soldier happened to look over my dad's shoulder to see the tender expressions of love he was communicating to my mom. *I'm*

21

as rough as ever might have been the most appropriate thing to write at that time!

I imagine those thoughts because I believe my mom was very much aware of Dad's beautiful combination of toughness and tenderness. He was a man's man. Strong. Powerful. Yet, tender. Gentle. Comforting. Soothing.

Loving People are Not Perfect, so a Sense of Humor is Essential.

I'm still as rough as ever, and I'd probably be pushing your nose—biting or twisting your arm around a bedpost—or even smashing your finger in a nutcracker if you were here right now. Ha!

As I read the lines Dad writes about the awkward accidents that occur between two people in love, I smile. First of all, who can't relate to that sort of thing? The flawless dance between man and woman is only portrayed in movies and romance novels. The rest of us are committed, yet clumsy.

The absolute best way to deal with the reality of our humanity is to include a large dose of laughter along with the unexpected incidences of life. Dad was generous with his humor—so much so that we'll look at his comic genius later in other chapters. One of his favorite words to write was 'Ha!'

Love is Like a Lovely Flower.

Love is like a lovely flower. You can look at it—smell it—adore it, but never abuse it or it will die.

What a stunning metaphor for the most beautiful of all emotions. I'm not sure Dad ever thought of himself as a poet or a philosopher, but with this picture he paints, he deserves to be considered as both.

Love is hard work. Love takes effort. Love requires intentional expression. But alongside those concepts, Dad understood that there is a tenderness to love. A soft, deep appreciation that transcends all other behaviors. Love requires that ingredient as much as it requires the others. You look at it, adore it and never abuse it.

Our flower has weathered the storm and spring frosts—it has blossomed into a beautiful flower with a little bud (Linda) for all to take notice of. When I'm with you I'm as happy as I can possibly be.

No marriage is perfect. My parents had their 'storms' and 'spring frosts' just like any other couple. But they hung in there. They stayed with it. Their faithful commitment to one another was etched in stone.

*   *   *

I would learn a great deal more on the subject of marriage through the years. Having access to Dad's letters to Mom helped enormously. But rising above them all was the letter that Dad wrote to me when I was only six years old.

Chapter Three

Open This Letter in Ten Years

In the world of art, music and literature, there is a Latin term known as *magnum opus*. It means 'a large and important work, especially regarded as the most important work of the artist or writer.'

When one considers all the letters Dad wrote home while he was in the Army, in my estimation, his Magnum Opus was not a love letter he wrote to his wife. It was a love letter he wrote to *me*. It certainly qualifies as a large work. But as you read it, you will see it also qualifies in its importance. Here it is in full:

10 Dec 1951
Tokarazowa Japan

Darling,

You were only six when I wrote this letter, but I felt the inspiration to write it for several reasons. One because we never know how long we are going to be around, and secondly because by the time you are sixteen I may be considered to be too old fashioned to think the youthful way I do now.

You're sixteen now and next fall you will be in your senior year in high school. After that it will mean college. I want to believe you are behaving Lin. You are sixteen now and that makes me a little late to discuss love and I'm too early to discuss sex, but there's a chance I'm right on time.

If I know your mother, she'd like to keep you right in the back yard until you are 23, then have you meet some nice boy and get married, all in one day. She thinks that's how it happened to us, and I'm glad. That proves she's forgotten all the fellows she knew before me, just as she made me forget the girls I knew before her.

Auctually it didn't work that way at all. There were others and they were important. Lin, love isn't spontaneous combustion. It's a matter of choice, a process of elimination. All those others are like preliminaries in the contest of finding the

26

person you want to marry.

I suspect you'll follow the same pattern. There was Jim and then Bob, and now Ed., and undoubtly a few others in between and many more ahead. You'll find yourself cutting down the list until you start returning again and again to a certain one because - somehow - he's got a grip on your heart, and you don't want him to let go.

Then you'll recognize each other and it'll seem you just met for the first time, and that there never was anyone else, that you never doubted each other. That's the idea your mother has, and it's a good idea if you can keep it alive.

You may think I'm premature Lin, to discuss marriage even before you have known love, but I don't know how to separate the two. Marriage evolves from love, and marriage can't succeed without love. The attitudes you're developing now towards the boys you know will establish the pattern of your conduct ~~too~~ towards your husband.

Marriage brought new, vital experiences to your mother and me. Now, we want to believe that it will likewise hold the same newness for you. I'm sure you understand that. I'm sure you've had your share of necking, — all I can hope is that you've learned by this time to know when

when a little fun approaches a dangerous precipice. What's the danger? Let me put it this way Lin. Virginity is the finest wedding gift a man and a woman can give each other. The danger, then, is that a moments enthusiasm can shatter everything we've tried to teach you at home and through the church, and it taints the heart which some splendid boy somewhere is waiting for you to offer him. That, whatever your hotshot friends may tell you to the contrary, is a definite loss, and a sad one.

I wish I could take all the ingredients for a successful marriage mix them, and say, "Here, Linda, here's happiness!" But thats not the way it happens, Lin. The ingredients are the same for every man and wife; it's the recipe that makes the difference. And that recipe is something each couple must work out for themselves.

I know it doesn't look that way from your side of the fence. After having a wonderful time on a date, you'll come home thinking you've just been deeded an acre of heaven. That's fine. And when you meet the boy you want to marry, you'll think God has given you the whole place, and there's no feeling in the world like that. You'll want to make that happiness a permanent part of your life, and thus you have it Linda.

that is the challenge of marriage.

Don't be surprised if a sudden fear almost scares you out of marriage at the last moment. Realizing you are about to make promises you must keep for the rest of your life is enough to frighten anybody. Your mother and I felt that on our wedding day. I remember telephoning her an hour before the ceremony.

Hello, are you alright? "Okay" she said – 'are you?'. I think there was hesitance in both our voices.

And so we met at the alter an hour later, still scared by the bigness of what we were beginning, and being afraid together only made us need each other more. I suspect we have always remained a little afraid. Marriage is a living thing, Linda, and as such it is subject to change. Being a little afraid is good, because it makes you eager to please, and any change that comes from that attitude can only be improvements.

But your marriage can go the other way, if you forget the man you marry will always remain an individual. When the two of you say "I do" you sign an alliance not a surrender.

Like all women, your mother thinks that she and I are not two separate people, but one soul inhabiting two bodies. That's a nice thought, Linda, but it couldn't be true for any married couple.

Nothing miraculous takes place when two people marry. A man and a woman who love each other merely announce to the world that they are going to take a chance at the tough job of living together harmoniously. They remain their separate selves, with their own opinions, their own whims, their own interests. The harmony results from — compromising those differences. And you can't ration those compromises. Out of your love you develop a sensitivity that tells you when either should step back.

Whether or not you obey that sensitivity decides how well you're going to get along.

All the problems of married life are simple if you approach them with your head as well as your heart.

You'll find yourself conceding many decisions to your husband, and you should. He needs that as an assurance of your confidence in him.

You'll find that in your desire to please your dates you will grow increasingly excited as the time for him to ring the door bell grows nearer. That is just a sample of what it will be like to have your husband return home each evening, and when that excitement fades, merely from time and habit, an important part of your happiness will die.

If you marry the right man Linda, you will never quite lose the quickening of your heart when you hear his footsteps, or his voice on the phone. The slightest reminder of him, just referring to him as "my husband," will hold a keen warm pleasure which never completely fades.

Little things. — but a happy marriage must have those minor miracles. You aren't in love only at Christmas or birthdays or anniversaries, — you're in love every minute, and 60 seconds is just enough time for hands to touch, for eyes to meet in a crowded room, for smiles to exchange a hundred secrets.

Sometimes the adjustments of being married
hits a snag. When that happens, Linda,
you're on your own. It's like standing at
the edge of a cliff with a strong wind at your
back. Then, for minutes, for hours, and
perhaps days, a little something nips at your
heart; but suddenly comes a rush of tears,
and babbled apologies, and you grab at
love with the violent relief that another of
life's big crises is over.

Sometimes you'll explode with love.
You'll want your husband with a fury that
makes you tremble, and the moments when
you share that hunger will be the heights
of your love. But don't expect that everytime.

You must realize that, if you want your
husband to look upon your private moments
as the beautiful moments they should be.
You must sense when he is ready to bring
you his own desires and when he merely
accepts yours. Aware of this difference, it becomes
your duty to sacrifice yourself for him.

Some women don't see it that way.
They resent that sacrifice and every compromise
they have to make. They go into marriage

blindly. They forget that it's success depends only on countless adjustment. And so they are susceptible to the first handsome man strolling by, who appears willing to demand less and give more than their husbands. Fidelity in my opinion is a law of conscience. It is an innate loyalty to ideals a man has all his life.

Right now you owe fidelity to your mother and me and all the things we've tried to teach you. You owe it to your country, your church, your school, your friends, and one day you will owe it to your husband. Infidelity is like committing treason against yourself. The haunting regret of it in marriage must be in realizing that a woman has looked away from the husband who trusts her, believes in her, and shares her darkest hours.

There can't be any happiness in that. Because of it, something that was intended to be good and beautiful becomes tainted, and there is no peace in knowing that you are guilty of distruction.

That's what I want you to remember, Linda,
above everything else, and then all the other
things will fall into place, just as I know
you want them to.

By far the grandest thrill of such a love
are the children who become part of your
family. The fullest moment of your life
will come the first time you look down
at the new baby. In that pink, wrinkled,
screeching bundle of humanity is the
fulfillment of all the dreams of your wedding
day, — the revival of the promises you made.
Suddenly you have a future, and it's
wrapped up in that miracle you call "My kid".
Then you will have everything, Linda.
— a husband, a family — a home. All
of it resulting from the wonderful accident
of one day meeting a man with whom
you exchanged pure hearts and shared ideals.
Remember, you have some glorious
adventures ahead of you Linda.

But there's one more thing. Your husband,
your family, your home — your entire life
can be truly valuable only if you have a
guest in your house, and that guest is God.

There's been too much happiness in our
home, Linda, for me to believe that you
and Mother and I have created it all by ourselves.
I think we've had some outside help. And if
our happiness is a reward from God for the
way we've lived, then I want you to go on as
we are living, because you deserve the same
happiness for your own home that you'll
start someday.

That's why I've written this letter Linda.
You'll find it waiting for you when you
are around 16 years old. I've tried to put
all the answers to a successful life for
you in this letter. Don't expect to grasp
the full meaning of it's contents the first
time you read it. Somewhere in this letter
you'll find the answer to all your problems.
Read it often.

Your loving father

10 December 1951

Tokarazowa, Japan

Darling,

You were only six when I wrote this letter, but I felt the inspiration to write it for several reasons. One, because we never know how long we are going to be around, and secondly because by the time you are sixteen I may be considered to be too old fashioned to think the youthful way I do now.

You're sixteen now and next fall you will be in your senior year in high school. After that it will mean college. I want to believe you are behaving, Lin. You are sixteen now and that makes me a little late to discuss love and I'm too early to discuss sex, but there's a chance I'm right on time.

If I know your mother, she'd like to keep you right in the back yard until you are 23, then have you meet some nice boy and get married, all in one day. She thinks that's how it happened to us, and I'm glad. That proves she's forgotten all the fellows she knew before me, just as she made me forget the girls I knew before her.

Actually it didn't work that way at all. There were others and they were important. Lin, love isn't spontaneous combustion. It's a matter of choice, a process of elimination. All those others are like preliminaries in the contest of finding the person you want to marry.

I suspect you'll follow the same pattern. There was Jim and then Bob and now Ed, and undoubtedly a few others in between and many more ahead. You'll find yourself cutting down the list until you start returning again and again to a certain one because—somehow—he's got a grip on your heart and you don't want him to let go.

Then you'll recognize each other and it'll seem you just met for the first time and that there never was anyone else, that you never doubted each other. That's the idea your mother has, and it's a good idea if you can keep it alive.

You may think I'm premature, Lin, to discuss marriage even before you have known love, but I don't know how to separate the two. Marriage evolves from love, and marriage can't succeed without love. The attitudes you're developing now towards the boys you know will establish the pattern of your conduct towards your husband.

Marriage brought new, vital experiences to your mother and me. Now, we want to believe that it will likewise hold the same newness for you. I'm sure you understand that. I'm sure you've had your share of necking—all I can hope is that you've learned by this time to know when a little fun approaches a dangerous precipice. What's the danger? Let me put it this way Lin. Virginity is the finest wedding gift a man and a woman can give each other. The danger, then, is that a moment's enthusiasm can shatter everything we've tried to teach you at home and through the church, and it taints the heart, which some splendid boy somewhere is waiting for you to offer him. That, whatever your hotshot friends may tell you to the contrary, is a definite loss, and a sad one.

I wish I could take all the ingredients for a successful marriage, mix them and say, "Here, Linda, here's happiness!" But that's not the way it happens, Lin. The ingredients are the same for every man and wife; it's the recipe that makes the difference. And that recipe is something each couple must work out for themselves.

I know it doesn't look that way from your side of the fence. After having a wonderful time on a date, you'll come home thinking you've just been deeded an acre of heaven. That's fine. And when you meet the boy you want to marry, you'll think God has given you the whole place, and there's no feeling in the world like that. You'll want to make that happiness a permanent part of your life, and there you have it Linda, that is the challenge of marriage.

Don't be surprised if a sudden fear almost scares you out of marriage at the last moment. Realizing you are about to make promises you must keep for the rest of your life is enough to frighten anybody. Your mother and I felt that on our wedding day. I remember telephoning her an hour before the ceremony.

"Hello, are you alright?" "Okay," she said. "Are you?" I think there was hesitance in both our voices.

And so we met at the altar an hour later, still scared by the bigness of what we were beginning and being afraid together only made us need each other more. I suspect we have always remained a little afraid. Marriage is a living thing, Linda, and as such it is subject to change. Being a little afraid is good, because it makes you eager to please and any change that comes from that attitude can only be improvements.

But your marriage can go the other way, if you forget the man you marry will always remain an individual. When the two of you say, "I do" you sign an alliance, not a surrender. Like all women, your mother thinks that she and I are not two separate people, but one soul inhabiting two bodies. That's a nice thought Linda, but it couldn't be true for any married couple.

Nothing miraculous takes place when two people marry. A man and a woman who love each other merely announce to the world that they are going to take a chance at the tough job of living together harmoniously. They remain their separate selves, with their own opinions, their own whims, their own interests. The harmony results from—compromising those differences. And you can't ration those compromises. Out of your love you develop a sensitivity that tells you when either should step back. Whether or not you obey that sensitivity decides how well you're going to get along. All the problems of married life are simple if you approach them with your head as well as your heart.

You'll find yourself conceding many decisions to your husband, and you should. He needs that as an assurance of your confidence in him.

You'll find that in your desire to please your dates you will grow increasingly excited as the time for him to ring the doorbell grows near. That is just a sample of what it will be like to have your husband return home each evening and when that excitement fades, merely from time and habit, an important part of your happiness will die.

If you marry the right man, Linda, you will never quite lose the quickening of your heart when you hear his footsteps, or his voice on the phone. The slightest reminder of him as "my husband" will hold a keen warm pleasure, which never completely fades.

Little things—but a happy marriage must have those minor miracles. You aren't in love only at Christmas or birthdays or anniversaries—you're in love every minute, and 60 seconds is just enough time for hands to touch, for eyes to meet in a crowded room, for smiles to exchange a hundred secrets.

Sometimes the adjustments of being married hit a snag. When that happens, Linda, you're on your own. It's like standing at the edge of a cliff with a strong wind at your back. Then for minutes, for hours, and perhaps days, a little something nips at your heart; but suddenly comes a rush of tears and babbled apologies and you grab at love with a violent relief that another of life's crises is over.

Sometimes you'll explode with love. You'll want your husband with a fury that makes you tremble, and the moments when you share that hunger will be the heights of your love. But don't expect that every time. You must realize that, if you

40

want your husband to look upon your private moments as the beautiful moments they should be. You must sense when he is ready to bring you his own desires and when he merely accepts yours. Aware of this difference, it becomes your duty to sacrifice yourself to him.

Some women don't see it that way. They resent that sacrifice and every compromise they have to make. They go into marriage blindly. They forget that its success depends only on countless adjustments. And so they are susceptible to the first handsome man strolling by, who appears willing to demand less and give more than their husbands. Fidelity in my opinion is a law of conscience. It is an innate loyalty to ideals a man has all his life.

Right now you owe fidelity to your mother and me and all the things we've tried to teach you. You owe it to your country, your church, your school, your friends and one day you will owe it to your husband. Infidelity is like committing treason against yourself. The haunting regret of it in marriage must be in realizing that a woman has looked away from the husband who trusts her, believes in her, and shares her darkest hours.

There can't be any happiness in that. Because of it, something that was intended to be good and beautiful becomes tainted, and there is no peace in knowing that you are guilty of destruction.

That's what I want you to remember, Linda, above everything else, and then all the other things will fall into place, just as I know you want them to.

By far the grandest thrill of such a love are the children who become part of your family. The fullest moment of your life will come the first time you look down at that new baby. In that pink, wrinkled screeching bundle of humanity is the fulfillment of all the dreams of your wedding day—the revival of promises you made.

Suddenly you have a future, and it's wrapped up in that miracle you call "My kid." Then you will have everything, Linda—a husband, a family—a home. All of it resulting from the wonderful accident of one day meeting a man with whom you exchanged pure hearts and shared ideals. Remember you have some glorious adventures ahead of you Linda.

But there's one more thing. Your husband, your family, your home—your entire life can be truly valuable only if you have a guest in your house and that guest is <u>God.</u> There's been too much happiness in our home, Linda, for me to believe that your mother and I have created it all by ourselves. I think we've had some outside help. And if our happiness is a reward from God for the way we've lived, then I want you to go on as we are living, because you deserve the same happiness in your own home that you'll start someday.

That's why I've written this letter, Linda. You'll find it waiting for you when you are around 16 years old. I've tried to put all the answers to a successful life for you in this letter. Don't expect to grasp the full meaning of its contents the first time you read it. Somewhere in this letter you'll find the answer to all your problems. Read it often.

Your loving father

Can you even imagine how special I felt to have a father who would go to such an effort to communicate so many good things to me about my future as a married woman?

There is so much to glean from these words that we need to break down Dad's Magnum Opus into several different chapters. Ready? Here we go.

Chapter Four

Love Isn't Spontaneous Combustion

Nineteen hundred and fifty-one.

What a year in the history of the United States.

President Truman and General MacArthur aren't seeing eye to eye on how to handle the Korean Conflict. Republicans finally convince Ike to run for President in '52. Senator McCarthy has been at it for over a year now, seeing Communists under every rock. The 22nd Amendment of the Constitution is passed, limiting the presidency to two terms. William J. Levitt, the developer of 'Levittown,' becomes the poster boy for human migration out of cities to the suburbs. Also, if you'd like, you can buy plans in order to build your own bomb shelter.

In baseball, it's an all–New York City affair. Bobby Thompson hits 'The Shot Heard Round the World,' off the Brooklyn Dodgers on October 3rd, putting his New York Giants into the World Series against the New York Yankees. The Yanks win the series 4 games to 2. In football, the Los Angeles Rams defeated the Cleveland Browns 24-17 for the NFL Championship.

It was a big year for movies. The Oscar for Best Picture went to *An American in Paris,* but the competition included *A Place in the Sun, Quo Vadis* and *A Streetcar Named Desire.* CBS premiered a news show called *See It Now,* with Edward R. Murrow. For laughs, there were programs like *The Jack Benny Show, The Red Skelton Show,* and of course, *I Love Lucy.* Television also provided pastoral opportunities for men like Billy Graham and Bishop Fulton J. Sheen. We were reading books by Herman Wouk, Mickey Spillane, Norman Mailer and William F. Buckley. The soundtrack of 1951 included Patti Page singing *Tennessee Waltz, How High the Moon* by Les Paul and Mary Ford, and *Too Young* by Nat King Cole.

In Cleveland, a radio disc jockey named Alan Freed started calling rhythm and blues records 'rock and roll.'

*   *   *

South about 72 miles down the road from Alan Freed's Cleveland is the little town of Sandyville, Ohio. You know Sandyville, don't you? It's right between Canton, Ohio and New Philadelphia, Ohio. It was kind of an Ohio version of Lake Wobegone. Sandyville is where my mom and I were living—in a small apartment above the Post Office in December of 1951 when Dad sent me his jewel from Japan.

Once again, here's how the letter begins:

10 December 1951

Tokarazowa, Japan

Darling,

You were only six when I wrote this letter, but I felt the inspiration to write it for several reasons. One, because we never know how long we are going to be around, and secondly because by the time you are sixteen I may be considered to be too old fashioned to think the youthful way I do now.

You're sixteen now and next fall you will be in your senior year in high school. After that it will mean college. I want to believe you are behaving, Lin. You are sixteen now and that makes me a little late to discuss love and I'm too early to discuss sex, but there's a chance I'm right on time.

If I know your mother, she'd like to keep you right in the back yard until you are 23, then have you meet some nice boy and get married, all in one day. She thinks that's how it happened to us, and I'm glad. That proves she's forgotten all the fellows she knew before me, just as she made me forget the girls I knew before her.

Actually it didn't work that way at all. There were others and they were important. Lin, love isn't spontaneous combustion. It's a matter of choice, a process of elimination. All those others are like preliminaries in the contest of finding the person you want to marry.

I suspect you'll follow the same pattern. There was Jim and then Bob and now Ed, and undoubtedly a few others in between and many more ahead. You'll find yourself cutting down the list until you start returning again and again to a certain one because—somehow—he's got a grip on your heart and you don't want him to let go.

Then you'll recognize each other and it'll seem you just met for the first time and that there never was anyone else, that you never doubted each other. That's the idea your mother has, and it's a good idea if you can keep it alive.

You may think I'm premature, Lin, to discuss marriage even before you have known love, but I don't know how to separate the two. Marriage evolves from love, and marriage can't succeed without love. The attitudes you're developing now towards the boys you know will establish the pattern of your conduct towards your husband.

Marriage brought new, vital experiences to your mother and me. Now, we want to believe that it will likewise hold the same newness for you. I'm sure you understand that. I'm sure you've had your share of necking—all I can hope is that you've learned by this time to know when a little fun approaches a dangerous precipice. What's the danger? Let me put it this way Lin. Virginity is the finest wedding gift a man and a woman can give each other. The danger, then, is that a moment's enthusiasm can shatter everything we've tried to teach you at home and through the church, and it taints the heart, which some splendid boy somewhere is waiting for you to offer him. That, whatever your hotshot friends may tell you to the contrary, is a definite loss, and a sad one.

I wish I could take all the ingredients for a successful marriage, mix them and say, "Here, Linda, here's happiness!" But that's not the way it happens, Lin. The ingredients are the same for every man and wife; it's the recipe that makes the difference. And that recipe is something each couple must work out for themselves.

I know it doesn't look that way from your side of the fence. After having a wonderful time on a date, you'll come home thinking you've just been deeded an acre of heaven. That's fine. And when you meet the boy you want to marry, you'll think God has given you the whole place, and there's no feeling in the world like that. You'll want to make that happiness a permanent part of your life, and there you have it Linda, that is the challenge of marriage.

There is so much to learn from this section of the letter. Here are a few of my favorite gems:

Give Your Child One of the Greatest Gifts You Can Offer

You were only six when I wrote this letter, but I felt the inspiration to write it for several reasons. One, because we never know how long we are going to be around, and secondly because by the time you are sixteen I may be considered to be too old fashioned to think the youthful way I do now.

Before we even dig into the letter's contents, consider the overall premise. Who takes the time to write a letter of this magnitude to a 6-year-old? In today's world of instant information, most people would just buy the kid a book or let him or her listen to a *Ted Talk* or watch a YouTube video to get the information that Dad so lovingly and painstakingly imparted in flawless longhand from a faraway distance.

Was the world really that different in 1951? How many people do you know who would take the time, effort and energy to compose a letter, written while the child is only 6, to be opened when she turns 16? It sounds like an alien universe to those of us in the 21st Century. This loving epistle came from quite a man!

We excuse ourselves, claiming the world is a much busier place than it was in 1951. That may be true, but wouldn't someone living in 1951 think his or her world was so much busier than it was in 1900?

One makes time for what that person views as important. Parents, as you read Dad's letter to me, perhaps it will motivate you to write a similar letter to your children, no matter what ages they may be. In doing so, you are giving them a priceless gift.

Love Isn't Spontaneous Combustion

Lin, love isn't spontaneous combustion. It's a matter of choice, a process of elimination. All those others are like preliminaries in the contest of finding the person you want to marry.

You may think I'm premature, Lin, to discuss marriage even before you have known love, but I don't know how to separate the two. Marriage evolves from love, and marriage can't succeed without love. The attitudes you're developing now towards the boys you know will establish the pattern of your conduct towards your husband.

Dad was so wise to let me in on one of love's big secrets—it's an evolving thing. There may be a long list of dates and boyfriends and crushes and infatuations that take place over time, but eventually you find the one you've been looking for.

And when it comes to love, it is a *choice*. It's an act of the will. I understand that some who read these words married the very first person they ever dated, and it's been a fulfilling relationship for a long time. But for the rest of us, Dad helped me to understand that finding the right person included what he referred to as 'a process of elimination.' That was truly helpful to me.

The ultimate way in which love grows is the way it can lead to marriage. "Marriage can't succeed without love," Dad knowingly counsels. The picture of a loveless marriage is one of the saddest images imaginable.

Virginity is The Finest Wedding Gift

Virginity is the finest wedding gift a man and a woman can give each other. The danger, then, is that a moment's enthusiasm can shatter everything we've tried to teach you at home and through the church, and it taints the heart, which some splendid boy somewhere is waiting for you to offer him. That, whatever your hotshot friends may tell you to the contrary, is a definite loss, and a sad one.

I know, I know, this is very 1950s in its thinking. So much has changed in our culture since these words of wisdom were offered. Many people have come full circle, believing the more experienced you are as you enter marriage, the better off you will be.

But maybe Dad is not as out of touch as one might think.

The therapist's notebooks are filled with the musings of patient after patient lamenting the dysfunction occurring in a current relationship that has its roots in a prior relationship. These issues can be worked through, but why put yourself in the situation initially that creates that situation?

The Ingredients are the Same, It's the Recipe that's Unique

I wish I could take all the ingredients for a successful marriage, mix them and say, "Here, Linda, here's happiness!" But that's not the way it happens, Lin. The ingredients are the same for every man and wife; it's the recipe that makes the difference. And that recipe is something each couple must work out for themselves.

Dad was insightful enough to understand that every married couple takes the same ingredients and mixes them up in their own exquisite entrée. Especially when one remembers that these words are being written in 1951, when there was more of a cookie cutter approach to marriage, these thoughts are not only brilliant, but clearly ahead of their time.

My own marriage is the perfect example. Bob and I have been married for over 50 years now. And we've been happily married! Our success in marriage has a lot to do with learning to apply many of the pieces of advice we were given by my dad. But having said that, here's what's noteworthy. Bob and Linda's marriage is different from Tony and Helen's marriage. Both happy, but definitely distinct from one another.

That's why I love the metaphor Dad uses in his letter—the same ingredients but different recipes. You can't be Italian without having a love affair with food. And it really helps if you learn how to cook it well.

Take lasagna, for instance. We all make it with the same ingredients, but you can get a different taste every time based on the use of those ingredients. A little more spice, a little less cheese, the consistency of the red sauce—the chef makes the decisions, and the perfect dish is served. (Just make sure it's not overcooked!)

As a good Italian Catholic, Dad was aware of a fundamental teaching in Catholic theology…

…If you overcook pasta, you will go straight to Hell.

So, Mom had to learn how to cook—a necessary adjustment to avoid the snag that could end up as a crisis. We will develop that further in the next chapter.

God knew what He was doing when He put Bob and Linda together and when He put Tony and Helen together. He's the Master Chef!

Chapter Five

Compromising Your Differences

My mother had an adventurous spirit about her from her earliest recollections of life. She grew up in a family of seven siblings, an adventure she shared with my dad. Unlike Dad, she grew up on a farm, an adventure she undertook along her own unique pathway.

Growing up on a farm was okay, but the life among the crops and the cows left Helen wanting more. At 16, she left home, heading towards the big city of Canton. Left behind were her family and her education. She would never complete high school.

Canton was beckoning and once she succumbed to its siren call, Helen knew right away she needed a job in order to survive. So, she began as a waitress at an upscale Canton restaurant known as The Onesto, snugly tucked into the impressive Onesto Hotel, a fourteen story Canton icon on the corner of Cleveland Avenue and Second Street NW. She was able to get to work each day on public transportation, but getting back home after work was another story.

She always needed a ride home.

The story is told of the time a handsome young gentleman was dining at the restaurant and he struck up a conversation with the beautiful and hardworking waitress (that's Mom). All was well. Somewhere in the chit-chat, it came out that Helen needed a ride home. "I'd be glad to take you home," volunteered the handsome young gentleman. My mother smiled sweetly and accepted his kind invitation.

However, the handsome young gentleman had other ideas as he drove Helen away from The Onesto. "I need to stop by my apartment," he announced, much to my mother's consternation. She had been warned about these sorts of shenanigans before. She hoped for the best but planned for the worst.

Unfortunately, the worst is what she got.

Reluctantly, she agreed to accompany the gentleman into his apartment. Once inside, it was crystal clear that he had no intention of taking her home in the immediate future. Helen insisted that she be driven home right away. First, she spoke softly and kindly. Then, she added greater volume and depth to her voice. No matter her tone, the man (he had gone from 'gentleman' to 'man' right before her eyes) refused to comply.

As soon as Helen realized this jerk (see how quickly the descriptions deteriorate) was not going to take her home, she stepped up her game a notch or two in order to make her point in a more dramatic fashion…

…Coolly and calmly, she strode over to the windows and began *setting the drapes on fire.*

The stupid jerk took her home.

*   *   *

The combustible curtains solved the immediate issue for Helen, but the fact still remained that she needed a ride home from work on a regular basis. On another night at The Onesto, another handsome young gentleman was enjoying a meal at one of Helen's tables. He was a soldier, home on leave from his military post with the Army Corps of Engineers. Unlike the previous diner, this soldier was a true gentleman. And so handsome! When he offered Helen a ride back to her place, she happily accepted his invitation.

He drove her straight home.

And that's how Helen Berry met Tony Sturrett.

They were married on April 8, 1944. Although based on this part of the letter he wrote me, it looks like they shared a dose of 'cold feet' on that April day.

Don't be surprised if a sudden fear almost scares you out of marriage at the last moment. Realizing you are about to make promises you must keep for the rest of your life is enough to frighten anybody. Your mother and I felt that on our wedding day. I remember telephoning her an hour before the ceremony.

"Hello, are you alright?" "Okay," she said. "Are you?" I think there was hesitance in both our voices.

And so we met at the altar an hour later, still scared by the bigness of what we were beginning and being afraid together only made us need each other more. I suspect we have always remained a little afraid. Marriage is a living thing, Linda, and as such it is subject to change. Being a little afraid is good, because it makes you eager to please and any change that comes from that attitude can only be improvement.

But your marriage can go the other way, if you forget the man you marry will always remain an individual. When the two of you say, "I do" you sign an alliance, not a surrender. Like all women, your mother thinks that she and I are not two separate people, but one soul inhabiting two bodies. That's a nice thought Linda, but it couldn't be true for any married couple.

Nothing miraculous takes place when two people marry. A man and a woman who love each other merely announce to the world that they are going to take a chance at the tough job of living together harmoniously. They remain their separate selves, with their own opinions, their own whims, their own interests. The harmony results from—compromising those differences. And you can't ration those compromises. Out of your love you develop a sensitivity that tells you when either should step back. Whether or not you obey that sensitivity decides how well you're going to get along. All the problems of married life are simple if you approach them with your head as well as your heart.

You'll find yourself conceding many decisions to your husband, and you should. He needs that as an assurance of your confidence in him.

You'll find that in your desire to please your dates you will grow increasingly excited as the time for him to ring the doorbell grows near. That is just a sample of what it will be like to have your husband return home each evening and when that excitement fades, merely from time and habit, an important part of your happiness will die.

If you marry the right man, Linda, you will never quite lose the quickening of your heart when you hear his footsteps, or his voice on the phone. The slightest reminder of him as "my husband" will hold a keen warm pleasure, which never completely fades.

Little things—but a happy marriage must have those minor miracles. You aren't in love only at Christmas or birthdays or anniversaries—you're in love every minute, and 60 seconds is just enough time for hands to touch, for eyes to meet in a crowded room, for smiles to exchange a hundred secrets.

Sometimes the adjustments of being married hit a snag. When that happens, Linda, you're on your own. It's like standing at the edge of a cliff with a strong wind at your back. Then for minutes, for hours, and perhaps days, a little something nips at your heart; but suddenly comes a rush of tears and babbled apologies and you grab at love with a violent relief that another of life's crises is over.

Here are a few more golden nuggets from this middle portion of my letter from Dad:

Being A Little Afraid is Good

Being a little afraid is good, because it makes you eager to please and any change that comes from that attitude can only be improvement.

Lest you think of my dad as beyond human, I was so glad to see him write that there were some cold feet on the wedding day. They were 'scared by the bigness' of the occasion. That's something worth noting.

All of us have moments in our lives that will arouse the butterflies in our bellies. It can be signing on the dotted line for the purchase of your first home. It could be nervously opening that letter from the college to which you applied, hoping it's announcing your acceptance. It could be the eternal wait in the doctor's waiting room, hoping those test results come back the right way. And it could be the nervous walk down the aisle in your long white gown—knowing it's right, but a battalion of butterflies command your attention.

Being a little afraid is good. It accentuates the importance of the event. We see this all the time in sporting events. My dad loved golf. I can see him on the 18th green, putting for the victory over his friendly competitors. That final putt is different than any other putt he would make that day. Why? Because it's for all the marbles. That putt requires more concentration, more discipline, more confidence than any other. And that touch of nerves that accompany it is just another reminder of its significance.

Dad is right—being a little afraid is good.

The Key to Two Becoming One—Compromising Your Differences

Nothing miraculous takes place when two people marry. A man and a woman who love each other merely announce to the world that they are going to take a chance at the tough job of living together harmoniously. They remain their separate selves, with their own opinions, their own whims, their own interests. The harmony results from—compromising those differences.

Any marriage and family therapist worth their salt will tell you that even though we are often attracted to our mate because of our mutual likes, it is the differences that bring the heat and energy to our relationship. 'Opposites attract' is true for many, but even if you married your clone, eventually you discover divergence.

How does a couple manage the differences? Dad's answer is right on. *Compromise.*

Rather than 'standing your ground' and creating greater disharmony, the better mode is for each of you to move towards the middle, towards each other. Instead of a tug of war, where each of you are straining to pull the other person over to your side, think of it as both of you on either end of the rope, placing hand over hand as you both move closer to the rope's center spot. When you meet there, you are experiencing the wisdom of compromising.

Little Things are Minor Miracles

Little things—but a happy marriage must have those minor miracles. You aren't in love only at Christmas or birthdays or anniversaries—you're in love every minute, and 60 seconds is just enough time for hands to touch, for eyes to meet in a crowded room, for smiles to exchange a hundred secrets.

Love and marriage are a 24/7 operation. As special as it is to get all dressed up and go out to celebrate an anniversary or other holiday, it's more about the gentle touch, the passing glance, and my favorite of Dad's expressions, 'smiles to exchange a hundred secrets.' Those smiles aren't limited to dress up affairs. Those smiles can occur when your hands are caked with inky black soil, as you've been weeding together in the garden. Those smiles can occur when one partner transfers the dirty, stinky diaper to the other partner for permanent residence in the trashcan outside. Those smiles can occur when the workout just ended, and your sweaty body looks and smells not so nice.

Little things are minor miracles.

All Marriages Include Adjustments, Snags and Crises

Sometimes the adjustments of being married hit a snag. When that happens, Linda, you're on your own. It's like standing at the edge of a cliff with a strong wind at your back. Then for minutes, for hours, and perhaps days, a little something nips at your heart; but suddenly comes a rush of tears and babbled apologies and you grab at love with a violent relief that another of life's crises is over.

I'm so glad Dad included this passage in his letter to me. As I have been saying, I was blessed to grow up in a home where there appeared to be no strife. But if the truth is to be told, even Dad and Mom experienced 'adjustments, snags and crises.' I'm not saying that I'm glad they had these issues, but I am glad to know that even the finest of marriages deal with their stuff.

Disagreements can destroy. Dad's description of being on your own, out on the edge of a cliff, the wind blowing at your back is a picture of the pain. As hurting and harrowing and heartbreaking as that can be, the story does a 180-degree flip when apologies are 'babbled.' The flood of tears, the loving embrace, the 'violent relief' sends the message that the crisis has passed.

Thank you, Dad, for such wise counsel.

*   *   *

The birth of Tony and Helen's little baby girl could qualify as an 'adjustment, snag, or crisis.' I was a premature birth—three pounds—requiring additional care and hospitalization. Dad was on a base in Virginia, while Mom was home in Canton. The strain was even evident before I arrived.

Mom had a few dramatic episodes during her pregnancy. For example, Dad had been alerted that "It's time for Helen to go to the hospital" so he made it home to Canton in record time. Patiently and lovingly, he packed her and her things in their old beat-up car and proceeded to the hospital. When I say the car was 'beat up' I'm actually speaking of it in more glowing terms than was true. Among other maladies, the four tires were as bald as a Yul Brynner Barbershop Quartet.

So, in the midst of Dad's patient and loving ride to the hospital, the unthinkable occurred. BLAM! The sound of a tire blowing out, accompanied by the sudden swerve of the car, brought my dad to a place he had never been before—at least in front of my mom.

"#$%^&!" he bellowed, as my mom's face began to melt off, like in a cheap horror movie.

She had never heard Dad swear until that moment.

To top it off, the visit to the hospital was unnecessary. She wasn't in labor. It was a false alarm.

Looking back, I'd call that an adjustment, a snag and a crisis all rolled into one. But there was a happy ending.

Eventually their little baby girl was born.

A new tire was purchased for the car.

Dad stopped swearing.

Chapter Six

Your Fidelity, Your Future and Your Faith

For Dad, it was never about what a person said or did on the surface. Rather, it was always about looking deeper into his or her soul.

He drilled that point home to me time and time again. It was more important what was going on down deep inside than the outward fashions one may wear. If I close my eyes, I can still hear Dad's voice exhorting me with one of his favorite phrases: *Linda, you are becoming what you will be!* And he wasn't talking about clothes.

I grew up under Dad's watchful gaze and by the time I was a teenager, Dad was still keeping a pretty close eye on me. He was always quite observant of my behavior, as well as how I looked, who my friends were, my grades, and of course, who I dated. To be fair, as much as Dad instilled in me the importance of emphasizing the inside over the outside, he didn't want me to take that to an extreme. In other words, he wanted me to always look my best.

This created a dilemma for me. Being a teenager in the early 1960s meant getting used to some significant changes in the culture. For example, 'getting all dressed up' was giving way to 'relax, man, be cool.'

I remember well the night I had a date with a guy who could best be described as 'dreamy.' He looked just like Troy Donahue, the heartthrob from TV shows like *Hawaiian Eye* and *Surfside Six*. Tall, tan, wavy blonde hair, and oh those eyes!

Dad noticed how casual I was dressing for my upcoming date and decided he needed to make a point. When my date came to the front door, Dad sprinted to the front hall, yelling out, "I'll get it!" He reached the door ahead of me—I could smell his familiar Old Spice scent as I followed the same path. It was at that moment that I caught my first glimpse of Dad's outfit for the evening. He met my date dressed in an old, wrinkled sweatshirt and sweatpants, hair as uncombed and disheveled as one can imagine and he even confiscated one of my long necklaces, which he was now wearing around his neck.

"Hi, I'm Linda's Dad," he announced, as both my date and I wore dropped jaws and bugged eyes.

Needless to say, I learned to dress a little nicer after that memorable lesson in style.

*　　*　　*

Dad wanted the best for me. In every area of my life. That's why he wrote of so many different subjects with such depth and compassion in his letter of 1951. Here's another section:

Sometimes you'll explode with love. You'll want your husband with a fury that makes you tremble, and the moments when you share that hunger will be the heights of your love. But don't expect that every time. You must realize that, if you want your husband to look upon your private moments as the beautiful moments they should be. You must sense when he is ready to bring you his own desires and when he merely accepts yours. Aware of this difference, it becomes your duty to sacrifice yourself to him.

Some women don't see it that way. They resent that sacrifice and every compromise they have to make. They go into marriage blindly. They forget that its success depends only on countless adjustments. And so they are susceptible to the first handsome man strolling by, who appears willing to demand less and give more than their husbands. Fidelity in my opinion is a law of conscience. It is an innate loyalty to ideals a man has all his life.

Right now you owe fidelity to your mother and me and all the things we've tried to teach you. You owe it to your country, your church, your school, your friends and one

67

day you will owe it to your husband. Infidelity is like committing treason against yourself. The haunting regret of it in marriage must be in realizing that a woman has looked away from the husband who trusts her, believes in her, and shares her darkest hours.

There can't be any happiness in that. Because of it, something that was intended to be good and beautiful becomes tainted, and there is no peace in knowing that you are guilty of destruction.

That's what I want you to remember, Linda, above everything else, and then all the other things will fall into place, just as I know you want them to.

By far the grandest thrill of such a love are the children who become part of your family. The fullest moment of your life will come the first time you look down at that new baby. In that pink, wrinkled screeching bundle of humanity is the fulfillment of all the dreams of your wedding day—the revival of promises you made.

Suddenly you have a future, and it's wrapped up in that miracle you call "My kid." Then you will have everything, Linda—a husband, a family—a home. All of it resulting from the wonderful accident of one day meeting a man with whom you exchanged pure hearts and shared ideals. Remember you have some glorious adventures ahead of you Linda.

But there's one more thing. Your husband, your family, your home—your entire life can be truly valuable only if you have a guest in your house and that guest is God. There's been too much happiness in our home, Linda, for me to believe that your mother and I have created it all by ourselves. I think we've had some outside help.

And if our happiness is a reward from God for the way we've lived, then I want you to go on as we are living, because you deserve the same happiness in your own home that you'll start someday.

That's why I've written this letter, Linda. You'll find it waiting for you when you are around 16 years old. I've tried to put all the answers to a successful life for you in this letter. Don't expect to grasp the full meaning of its contents the first time you read it. Somewhere in this letter you'll find the answer to all your problems. Read it often.

Your loving father

Here are some additional issues worth some extended discussion:

Physical Intimacy Includes Sacrifice

Sometimes you'll explode with love. You'll want your husband with a fury that makes you tremble, and the moments when you share that hunger will be the heights of your love. But don't expect that every time. You must realize that, if you want your husband to look upon your private moments as the beautiful moments they should be. You must sense when he is ready to bring you his own desires and when he merely accepts yours. Aware of this difference, it becomes your duty to sacrifice yourself to him.

No topic was off limits with my dad. I imagine him, sitting at his desk in Japan, asking himself the question, "How can I talk to my little girl about 'the birds and the bees' when I am thousands of miles away?" It always seems to be an awkward conversation to instigate; therefore, many parents never have the courage to have it. It's ironic, that there are parents in the next room who won't discuss these issues with their kids, while my dad was willing to talk about it from halfway around the world.

Dad sensitively strikes a balance as he discusses a married couple's sexual relationship. There are occasions when a man and a woman unite that produce a mutual satisfaction that is nothing short of marvelous. However, there are other times when there is more interest from one partner than the other, or vice versa. "Aware of this difference, it becomes your duty to sacrifice yourself..." Dad exhorts. Why would you do that? I can think of at least three reasons: First, because you love your spouse. Another, more self-serving reason is that you will want your partner to do the same for you when the situation is reversed. Thirdly, when a couple is genuinely growing in their love, giving of themselves is not viewed as a 'duty' but a joy.

Faithfulness is of Utmost Importance

Fidelity in my opinion is a law of conscience. It is an innate loyalty to ideals a man has all his life.

Once again, this may appear as very old fashioned, but I believe like Dad did—human beings are wired for monogamy. However, this is not the message one will receive from today's culture. I have a friend who recently said to me, "I binged watched the TV show *Mad Men* the other day. I'm only just beginning the third season and the main character, Don Draper, has already slept with six women other than his wife." Then she added, "And what's really crazy is that all the women in the show want to be with him and all the men in the show want to *be* him."

The *Playboy* philosophy of the wandering eye, the sleeping around, the thrill of the conquest perhaps makes for a good plot in a soap opera or a James Bond movie, or a trashy novel, but for real live human beings who live it, there is a hunger in the heart that infidelity cannot satisfy.

Many people talk about the excitement of the 'wild life', but few talk about the resulting pain.

The Fullest Moment of Your Life—Having A Child

By far the grandest thrill of such a love are the children who become part of your family. The fullest moment of your life will come the first time you look down at that new baby. In that pink, wrinkled screeching bundle of humanity is the fulfillment of all the dreams of your wedding day—the revival of promises you made.

My parents were great parents. Kind. Loving. Thoughtful. Self-sacrificing. Always wanting the best for me. In Dad's letter we can catch a glimpse of why he was such a good parent. It's the "fulfillment of all the dreams…"

It's a proud moment for a son or daughter when they hear Mom and Dad talk about the first time they saw their new baby. We are all born with an intense desire to *belong*. Hearing about the events surrounding our birth, especially the accompanying joy and celebration is a wonderful way to bring self-esteem to a child.

Only God Can Make a House a Home

But there's one more thing. Your husband, your family, your home—your entire life can be truly valuable only if you have a guest in your house and that guest is <u>God</u>. There's been too much happiness in our home, Linda, for me to believe that your mother and I have created it all by ourselves. I think we've had some outside help. And if our happiness is a reward from God for the way we've lived, then I want you to go on as we are living, because you deserve the same happiness in your own home that you'll start someday.

This point is an important one to Dad. It's so important that I want to save it for a later chapter where we can give it more detailed attention.

*   *   *

Wow. That was quite a letter, wouldn't you agree? Here's a summary of the points we highlighted from Dad's Magnum Opus:

Give Your Child One of the Greatest Gifts You Can Offer

Love Isn't Spontaneous Combustion

Virginity is The Finest Wedding Gift

The Ingredients are the Same, It's the Recipe that's Unique

Being A Little Afraid is Good

The Key to Two Becoming One—Compromising Your Differences

Little Things are Minor Miracles

All Marriages Include Adjustments, Snags and Crises

Physical Intimacy Includes Sacrifice

Faithfulness is of Utmost Importance

The Fullest Moment of Your Life—Having A Child

Only God Can Make a House a Home

*   *   *

Dad had a lot more to say about a variety of topics that were important to him. Let's widen our net here and catch a few more passions that were deep in the heart of Tony Sturrett.

Chapter Seven

A Crying Need at An Orphanage

If you look up the word *sportsman* in the dictionary, it will say, *'someone who participates in sporting activities, someone who competes in athletics.'*

Next to that definition would be a picture of Tony Sturrett.

Dad was a sportsman.

I've already mentioned Dad's love of golf. Not only did he love the game, he played it well. Like 'scratch golfer' well. But Dad's love of sports was not limited to golf. He loved them all.

Dad loved football. Growing up, he played it from the time he was a child, both at South Market Grade School and McKinley High School. McKinley was famous for many state football championships with a graduating class of over 2000.

Right out of high school he was offered and accepted an athletic scholarship from Southwest Missouri State Teachers College (known now as Missouri State University). They brought him in to play football! Even though he was considered to be on the short side, he was as explosive as a cannon ball. He played there for a year before moving back closer to home and attending Ohio University.

He was a linebacker for the semi-pro football team, the Downtown Eagles. They played at Dueber Field and you could watch them if you paid the admission--50 cents.

He also loved baseball, as well as boxing. There was a time in his youth when he became a boxing referee—I guess he did it to get even closer to the action. It was an ideal job for him, and he was the perfect referee because 1. He understood boxing from the boxer's standpoint, 2. He was honest, and 3. He was fair.

His other pursuits included a season of his life when he was committed to playing pool. It was not something that went over well with his mother. She was worried sick about him—after all, billiards was the sport of troubled youth. (As the song from *The Music Man* would put it: *You've got Trouble, Trouble, Trouble, with a capital T and that rhymes with P and that stands for Pool.*)

Dad never outgrew his love for sports, not only as a participant, but also as a fan. When I think back over my adolescent years, I remember quite vividly being taken along (I called it being 'dragged') to every boxing match for which Dad could get tickets. He especially loved watching baseball, played by his favorite team, the Cleveland Indians. Just like boxing matches, I accompanied Dad to more Tribe games than can be counted. We cheered especially loud for our favorite player, Rocky Colavito.

If you wanted to engage Dad in a lively conversation, all you had to do was ask him about Paul Brown or Joe Paterno and their football finesse. Or Joe DiMaggio and Larry Doby and their baseball brilliance. Or Joe Lewis as boxing's best. And of course, don't forget Sam Snead and Jack Nicklaus, golf's greatest.

When he couldn't attend the games, he took advantage of every other conceivable method of staying connected with the sports world. It may look like an exaggeration, but I can honestly remember observing my Dad watching a game on television, while listening to another game through the earpiece connected to his transistor radio, while scouring the sports page of the newspaper during commercials. All that was missing was handling a sports ticker tape with his toes. That's a committed fan.

*   *   *

During his stint in the Army, Dad completed part of his service at Fort Belvoir, in Virginia. It was a logical place for Dad to serve, since his area of expertise was engineering. The history of Fort Belvoir is a fascinating one. Here's how one source summarized it:

The post was founded during World War I as Camp A.A. Humphreys, named for American Civil War General Andrew A. Humpreys, who was also Chief of Engineers. The post was renamed Fort Belvoir in the 1930s in recognition of the Belvoir Plantation that once occupied the site. The adjacent United States Army Corps of Engineers Humpreys Engineer Center retains part of the original name.

Camp Humpreys was established in World War I as the U.S. Army Engineers Training School. It served as the post-graduate institution for U.S. Military Academy engineers and a finishing school for engineering troops heading to war. The school, which came to host the Engineer Officer Basic Course, relocated in 1988 from Fort Belvoir to Fort Leonard Wood in Missouri.[1]

We'll talk more about Dad's engineering adventures in a later chapter, but for now, it is important to note that the base is less than 20 miles from our nation's capital, Washington, D.C.

In the spring of 1945, right after I was born, Dad wrote home to Mom with the details of a secret mission in which he was involved. Truly a covert operation, this is how he described the incident to his wife:

---

[1] Fort Belvoir. www.Wikipedia.org

Darling,

I'm well aware that there are two women in my life now, but neither of them are going to be nagging because I will take immediate action to prevent such a thing. First, I will make you stand in the corner and next I will put a gag around Linda's mouth. Ha! I'll show you both who's boss.

Today I read in the paper that there is a crying need for athletic equipment at an orphanage in Washington. It seems that everything's being sold to the Army and Navy and nothing is available to these kids. I can easily remember as a child how much I enjoyed a baseball glove or a ball of any sort. I talked to a few higher ups about giving some stuff to these kids, but everyone turned me down, because Army regulations make no provision for donations. I decided to take matters into my own hands again. I made up a box and sent it to them anyway. I didn't tell them where it came from, because it's not legal, but they got the stuff and that's all I cared about anyway. I sent them ball bats, 1 dozen softballs, 6 pairs of boxing gloves, 4 pairs of horseshoes, badminton sets, several tennis rackets, baseballs, basketballs, footballs, volleyballs, medicine balls, chicken games, etc. I hope it will make these kids as happy as it made me as a kid to have something like this.

It was swell to talk to you tonight, darling.

All my love,

Pop

In my mind's eye I can see my dad grinning from ear to ear, knowing in his heart that a group of kids just twenty miles away now had the sports equipment they needed to live life the way he did as a child. He didn't even need to see it. Knowing it in his heart was good enough.

We can debate the merits of a man sending some things to a group of underprivileged kids that were meant for the Army all day long. And I'm sure I'm not the most objective judge in this instance, but I will tell you without hesitation that my dad had a heart as big as God makes them and in that big heart of his, it was the right thing to do.

What a profound lesson to learn from your father—practicing the gift of generosity. That was a trait that characterized my dad for as long as I knew him. Whether flush with cash or down to his last dime, Dad was a giver, not a taker.

What makes this lesson even more powerful is the fact that the Sturretts were far from wealthy. I can vividly recall a time when my dad was down to his last twenty dollars. What did he do? He gave five of it to someone in greater need.

If we reduced love down to the math, the question we all should ask is this one...

...*What would I do with my last twenty dollars?*

Chapter Eight

Right Down In The Mud With Them

Dad had attended the Southwest Missouri State Teachers College on a football scholarship, but after one year, he transferred to Ohio University to be closer to home. His program of study was engineering, a subject he took to quickly and with his normal degree of passion. He loved it. He excelled at it. Of course, his plan was to graduate with his engineering degree. But then, Dad became aware of a higher calling.

It was 1941. Like many brave men at that time, Dad willingly dropped out of college in order to enlist in the military.

After his years in the service, Dad never went back to finish his degree. His older brother, Joe, had completed his degree in civil engineering and began his own business, inviting my dad to join him. Technically, Dad was described as a 'non-degreed civil engineer', but he was neck deep in projects for roads and bridges, right by his brother Joe's side.

When one hears the title 'engineer,' one might imagine the stereotypical person who is quieter and more withdrawn, an introvert pouring over the plans and blueprints at a drafting table over in the corner of the room, rather than freely socializing with a crowd.

Dad did not fit that stereotype.

Even though he was exceptionally gifted in the engineering world, Dad was a people person. It's part of what made him a good leader. His years in the military provided numerous illustrations of both sides of his leadership coin. On one side, he had a heart for his men, constantly looking at ways to build up their morale. On the other side, he was a good engineer, and the Army Corps of Engineers was grateful to have him on their team.

We'll look at his love for his men in this chapter and then we'll flip the coin and look at his engineering competence in the next.

My Darling Wife,

You've got some more reason to be happy today. After several days of debating I was chosen for the job. Evidently my record held up. Does that make you happy?

The job is a big one until such time as I get it organized. My new title is A.S.F.T.C. Special Service Officer. I'm on the staff of the Post Commander. He has given me a free hand on organization. My biggest duty will be morale. It seems that the morale among overseas returnees is very poor. I'm to organize and put into effect athletic and social programs that are supposed to improve the morale of all the enlisted men on the post. The program hasn't been too effective and I fully intend to change things immediately. I'm going to concentrate my efforts on a widespread program of boxing matches, ball tournaments, tennis matches, dances, parties, musicals, and everything else that may improve morale—because if I'm successful it'll mean I'll be here for some time.

One thing I'm going to do immediately is open up a gripe office. One where they can come in and let their hair out to me. From that I can do something about their individual problems. I hope it works.

Today being my last day in my old job I told Col. Hooper off. Boy, did we have a round. I told him that furthermore, since I'm on the General's staff, I'm going to do all I could to cause a change for the better.

Darling, I love you so very much and now I'm happy, because I'm going to be here when you have the baby. Won't it be wonderful?

I'm enclosing your check of $200. Darling, let me know what the doctor said to you the last time you went to see him.

I'm so excited about the new job that I can't think of much else to say.

I guess the best thing I can say is just plain "I love you."

Give my regards to all.

All my love,

Pop

X x

If I'm in the military, I want to serve under this guy.

Boxing matches, ball tournaments, tennis matches, dances, parties, musicals, and everything else that may improve morale. Think about what that list of activities must have meant to the men under his command! And then, on top of that, add the 'gripe office.' Who gets to let someone know what's bothering him in a military setting? Well, in Dad's outfit, that's the way they did it.

I'm guessing that his intentions paid off and his men's morale greatly increased. There's a lesson there for every leader, be it leading troops, employees, or family.

Here's another example of Dad's commitment to the morale of his men:

Darling,

I just received your six letters. They were all swell—every one of them.

I'm going crazy today, honey. I'm firing 200 men that we've spent 6 weeks teaching how to shoot. This time they are firing for record.

Ordinarily I'd bet anyone that these men would fire as well as any I've ever taught, but today everything is against us. It rained all night and it's been raining all day so far today. The men are very cold, wet and muddy. I've done everything I could to bring their morale up. I got right down in the mud with them and ruined a $40 trench coat and an $18 pair of pants. I bought them $25 worth of hot dogs, $10 worth

83

of candy bars. I sang songs for them. I've told jokes to make them laugh and now it's up to them. I've got 'em so they'd rather qualify on the range today than get a 30 day furlough. They're trying hard because they don't want to let me down. These G.I.s are sure swell guys. I tried from 6:00 this morning to get their morale up, and just one hour ago they were trying to get mine up. One little fellow who is 18 years old was shivering cold and very uncomfortable, but he smiled when I approached him. I put my arm around his shoulders (he weighs 116 lbs.) and asked him how he was doing. He smiled in his childish way (he's so young, he's cute) and said, "Sir, anyone can shoot when the sun is shining, but it takes a real good man to shoot when it's bad weather. I'll prove I'm a good man," he said. Swell kid, huh?

I must close now. I must get back to the range. I've got to beat a certain Captain who has been praying for rain, as it will make it more difficult for my company to have the best score. My company holds the best record at the range, always shooting over 90%. His company is at a score of 89% and he is sure the rain will ensure that his company will win! The stinker.

I miss you awfully darling.

Love,

Tony

Dad's philosophy of leadership did not arrive from the 'Ivory Tower'. No, Dad got right down in the mud with them. Even if it cost him the price of a new coat and slacks. Even if he bought them extra food out of his own pocket. Even if he played the fool with his silly songs and his corny jokes. There was a comradery there that can only result from working together, shoulder to shoulder.

The end goal? *I've got 'em so they'd rather qualify on the range today than get a 30 day furlough. They're trying hard because they don't want to let me down.* The loyalty that is born at this level can only be described as respect. Dad knew that if he did all those things with his men and for his men, that they would respond with passion because they admired him.

It is so poignant that he included in his letter the story of that one G.I. in particular. The soldier is 18 years old and the way Dad describes him, I see him as looking more like he's 14. He weighs 116 pounds—I see a wisp of a boy with skin as white as vanilla ice cream, sprinkled with a large dose of freckles, topped with a dollop of orange-red hair. He's a skinny one. If he took his shirt off, you could count his ribs and see his heart thump in his chest. He tries his best to stay motionless, but the rain has created a cold deep inside him, and the shivering is involuntary. As he clutches his firearm, one is afraid that the weight of it will knock him over, if not by simply holding it, then surely when he fires it. He smiles at my dad in his childish way—*he's so young, he's cute.* This boy looks less like a soldier and more like the president of the eighth-grade chess club. Through that awkward, innocent looking smile, we hear his voice, cracking, as it has not yet fully changed into the sound of a man. *"Sir, anyone can shoot when the sun is shining, but it takes a real good man to shoot when it's bad weather. I'll prove I'm a good man."*

That kid became a good man.

Because he was led by a good man.

That kid admired my dad.

Because Dad respected that kid.

*   *   *

To me, that one young soldier represents every man my dad ever led. With my active imagination, I am envisioning whatever became of that scrawny little soldier. As the years went on, he matured into a fine young man. After his military service, perhaps he went back home to his small hometown and took over the family business for his dad. His employees grew to admire him because of the way he treated them. Or maybe he went to college on the G.I. Bill and became a high school history teacher, who also coached the track team. Those students loved his classes and his athletic teams pursued excellence. Life could have taken a hard turn for him—he could have come home seriously injured.

But his attitude for life could not be dimmed, for he had learned the advantage of a positive attitude.

It's even possible that this gawky teenager left the service, filled with a new love for and commitment to his country and began taking baby steps towards a life of public service. He could have become the mayor of a small town, or a county commissioner, or maybe even a state legislator.

Any of these results could have occurred. And a lot of it would have been due to a leader who respected his men and built their morale.

What was Dad's secret? What were the keys to his effective leadership?

Silly songs and corny jokes and $25 worth of hot dogs.

Demonstrating his great respect for the men in his command and wanting them to be their very best.

And, most importantly, getting right down in the mud with them.

Chapter Nine
Be Prepared

The Sturretts didn't let life dictate a script to them. Whenever possible, they wrote their own. In the United States, it started right off at Ellis Island. No longer were they to be known as the Sturiales, like they were back in Sicily. Instead, they changed their surname to Sturrett.

As a result of his elders' take-charge attitude, Dad learned to be prepared at a very early age. Growing up in an Italian family with four brothers and two sisters required a man with a plan, especially at the dinner table.

Dad was in the middle of the family birth order—fourth out of seventh. That can be a tough spot. It usually meant you didn't get the respect awarded to the oldest, or the extra attention bestowed on the youngest in the family. You had three others ahead of you, most often taking a large portion of the tastiest food on the dinner platter before it made its way to you. That's a man who needed a plan.

Carl was the oldest sibling, followed by Joe. Third in line was the first daughter, Conchetta, better known as Connie. Dad was next and then Angie. (Of all the siblings, Angie was most like Dad). Johnny was next and the youngest was Angelo, the baby of the bunch.

Years later, as the children grew to adulthood, it came time for the oldest daughter, Connie, to find a husband. No problem. Consider it handled. A plan was put in place. What did it look like? The family all agreed that the best place to find a good Italian husband for their Sweet Conchetta was back in Italy itself. So, two of the brothers, Carl and Joe, made the trip back to Sicily to interview prospective husbands for their sis. As Connie reviewed the prospects of olive workers and lemon pickers, she had the distinction of blurting out an exclamation few of us would have ever said as part of our courtship:

"I'll take that one!", as she pointed to a lemon picker.

Granted, it's not the way most of us found our life's partner, but I must tell you, Connie chose Sam Reale, who turned out to be the finest husband a woman could ever imagine.

*   *   *

Tony knew the value of planning ahead. It's the way he was brought up. And it was just that quality in his life that got him noticed at his post with the Army Corps of Engineers:

19 April 52

Hello Darling,

I got back from Muroran at 2:00 A.M. last night, and a car met me at the station. He had a note for me to attend a meeting at 8:00 A.M. in the Post Commander's Office to brief two new jobs (4 buildings and 5 sewage systems). Also to study the design and submit a cost estimate on 22 rifle and other gun ranges. I attended the meeting and met many Colonels and high ranking officers but none who would make a decision. I told them I was sent here to build things but that they would have to tell me their requirements before we could go ahead with design and building. I sounded angry. Especially when I said, "All this indecisiveness is only delaying the jobs you gentlemen require, and if none of you are prepared to make a decision on these ranges, there was no good reason to call this meeting. I must proportion my time among 19 projects, that in some cases are two days travel apart, and consequently my time is valuable." One Colonel asked me what I would do if I made the decision. Here's where I shined. I had prepared for this meeting and came with a sketch of what I would recommend. They all looked at it as I explained it. In fifteen minutes I convinced them it was the thing to do, and they all agreed. One Colonel from GHQ asked me to lunch, and said, "Sturrett, I like the way you made our decisions for us, and by the time you pulled out that sketch I could see you had intended to do exactly that before you came to the meeting." Ha! (He's right) He said, "I like the way you operate, and the way you speak for what you think is right regardless of the rank you are addressing— the Army needs more men like you." He offered me a job at GHQ in Tokyo. He was amazed when I told him I was a category IV involuntary recall and that I didn't want to change jobs because I liked my present job. He couldn't believe that I am not a professional engineer. He said, "You know so much about the construction you speak about that it doesn't seem possible that you are not really an engineer." Ha! What he doesn't know is that I spend hours studying the blue prints and specifications before I talk to anyone about any job. Which reminds me, I have four stacks of them here in my room right now that I'm going to take to bed with me and study instead of reading.

Good night darling. I'll answer all the questions in your letters in tomorrow's letter. I love you and Linda so much. There's no one like my little females. Give Linda my love and a great big kiss for me.

All my love,

Daddy

P.S. X x x

What a great example of how Dad lived his life. *I had prepared for this meeting and came with a sketch of what I would recommend.* Whether it was plans for a building or a bridge, or a husband for one of his sisters, or the discipline of writing to his bride every day they were apart, my dad was a

91

model of preparation. Certainly, there is something to be said for 'flying by the seat of your pants,' or 'winging it,' or 'making it up as you go along,' but I don't think the people who do that get as far along in life as those who take the time to carefully plan it out. It sure worked for Dad.

*   *   *

Many years later, when Dad returned to Canton, he found a barbershop that did a good job cutting his hair. Tony May, of Tony May's Barber Shop, would cut my dad's hair for the going price of the day—one dollar. Always planning ahead, Dad offered Tony a deal. "I'll pay you $2.50 for a haircut," Dad said. "But that's the price for the rest of my life." Tony shook Dad's hand, agreeing to the deal.

Now that it's all said and done, Dad paid $2.50 for a haircut for well over forty years. Sometimes Dad would visit Tony twice a week.

You have to admit, that was amazing foresight.

Chapter Ten

The King and the Captain:

"I Look Upon War With Horror"

I often thought of my dad as a king, most likely because he always treated me like a princess.

So, I found it to be extremely 'coincidental' (are there really 'coincidences' in life?) that as I was putting together my thoughts for this book in early 2020, I was made aware of a highly unusual event taking place. The Queen of England was set to deliver a brief, televised speech. Not an unusual circumstance in and of itself, her upcoming speech was especially significant since just a few weeks before she had spoken to her subjects about coping with the coronavirus, after having not been on TV for quite some time. Her upcoming speech would commemorate the 75th Anniversary of Victory in Europe Day (VE Day), May 8, 1945. The Queen was a princess back then, having just turned 19 less than three weeks earlier. Now at 94, a daughter was paying tribute to her father, just like I am doing with Dad.

May 8, 2020. At precisely 9:00 P.M. London time, the Queen began:

"I speak to you today at the same hour as my father did, exactly 75 years ago," the Queen said, seated comfortably in the White Drawing Room at Windsor Castle. One news source described the setting: *A photograph of King George VI in his Admiral of the Fleet uniform with RAF Wings was on the table next to the Queen during the broadcast. Placed to her other side was the cap she wore when she served in the Auxiliary Territorial Services during the Second World War, becoming the only female member of the royal family to join the Armed Forces as a full-time and active member. Behind her was a photograph of the royal family and Winston Churchill on the balcony of Buckingham Palace on VE Day.*[2]

The Queen continued: *"His message then was a salute to the men and women at home and abroad who had sacrificed so much in pursuit of what he rightly called a 'great deliverance.'*

"The war had been a total war; it had affected everyone and no one was immune from its impact.

[2] Murphy, Victoria. "Queen Elizabeth Pays Tribute to Her Father in a Moving Address to Mark the 75th Anniversary of VE Day." *Town & Country*, 8 May 2020, https://www.townandcountrymag.com/society/tradition/a32418712/queen-elizabeth-ve-day-anniversary-2020-speech-transcript/

'Whether it be the men or women called up to serve; families separated from each other; or people asked to take up new roles and skills to support the war effort, all had a part to play…

'We kept the faith that the cause was right—and this belief, as my father noted in his broadcast, carried us through.

'Never give up, never despair—that was the message of VE Day.

'I vividly remember the jubilant scenes my sister and I witnessed with our parents and Winston Churchill from the balcony of Buckingham Palace.

'The sense of joy in the crowds who gathered outside and across the country was profound, though while we celebrated the victory in Europe, we knew there would be further sacrifice.

'It was not until August that fighting in the Far East ceased and the war finally ended.

'Many people laid down their lives in that terrible conflict.

'They fought so we could live in peace, at home and abroad.

'They died so we could live as free people in a world of free nations.

'They risked all so our families and neighbourhoods could be safe.

'We should and will remember them.

"As I now reflect on my father's words and the joyous celebrations, which some of us experienced first-hand, I am thankful for the strength and courage that the United Kingdom, the Commonwealth and all our allies displayed.

95

"The wartime generation knew that the best way to honor those who did not come back from the war, was to ensure that it didn't happen again."

*   *   *

I find the parallels fascinating. Queen Elizabeth and Linda DeHoff are both reflecting on a time in the past when their fathers were not only alive and well, but strong, virile, 'large and in charge.' We both idolize our dads, as is evident by our loving words, communicated through letters, speeches and chapters of books.

Another part of this remarkable 'coincidence' is that earlier on the exact same day as the Queen's speech, I read a letter that Dad had written Mom regarding the identical occasion—VE Day! Dad put a bit of a different spin on the event. It's an important point of view to consider.

Sunday

My darling wife and daughter,

Millions of people all over the world breathe a little easier today—millions more will get drunk in celebration—V.E. day has officially arrived. The men who have fought so bravely in Europe will soon be coming home. At this point I thought that I would be one of the millions in celebration. I thought I would cheer and smile

96

genuinely for the first time in almost four long years, but somehow I can't. All I can think about is those that didn't make it. May their souls rest in peace. The pity of it is that soon the masses of people will forget the efforts of these dying heroes. The tyrants who escaped annihilation will begin to lay the foundation for a new war. Darling, I'm happy our child is a girl and sometimes I hope we never have a boy. War—in any form—is cruelty—and you can't refine it. I look upon war with horror and would not care for my son to take part in it.

There's a great peace conference going on in San Francisco right now. The fundamental principle laid down at that conference is to provide a just peace that will prevent future wars. I'm all for it and pray to God that the delegates can accomplish what they are so set on doing—but my familiarity with history tends to discount that such a thing is possible. Universal peace has been attempted before. Not too long ago President Wilson died in his efforts for universal peace. I'm afraid the same effort has killed Roosevelt. As long as little boys will fight, as they inevitably will, there will be wars.

I got a letter from Joe yesterday written from the place Ernie Pyle was killed. He says he's got a 30 day furlough and his is going to be assigned in the states. Isn't that wonderful?

I hope everything works out well for Joe up in N.Y. He's been away a long time and many changes could have taken place in his absence. He's experienced so many heartaches that I'm afraid for him if he should have to take another. Let's pray that everything turns out okay.

It's now 5:00 P.M. I'm going to have supper in a few minutes then go over to the telephone building and call you.

May God bless you always (Linda too)

Your loving husband,

Pop

There was no soldier prouder than my dad.

There was no soldier braver than my dad.

There was no soldier more committed than my dad.

Yet, in the midst of celebrating a great victory, Dad was painfully aware of the victory's cost. *All I can think about is those that didn't make it. May their souls rest in peace.* The conclusion of the agony of war brought a sobering silence instead of a satisfying smile.

My father's thoughts on this subject would prove to be a great help to me as I grew up. When the war in Vietnam put a chokehold on the world in the 1960s, it was popular to divide the United States into two factions—Hawks and Doves. The Doves were best characterized by the Hippies, protesting by demonstrations while carrying signs that would say *Make Love, Not War.* The Hawks were considered more a part of the Establishment—older folks who were the targets of sentiments like *Don't Trust Anyone Over 30.*

One doesn't need to think too long about which group my dad would choose. He was a true patriot who loved his country and was willing to fight for its freedoms. Yes, Dad was a Hawk.

But that's why this particular letter is so important. Being a Hawk doesn't mean you don't view war as a horrible thing. Like Dad wrote: *War—in any form—is cruelty—and you can't refine it. I look upon war with horror and would not care for my son to take part in it.*

*   *   *

Dad knew that war demanded sacrifice. And it was a sacrifice that was not only required of the soldiers, but the folks at home as well. He addressed this issue in a letter to my mom a year before they were married.

February 26, 1944

Darling,

I know and fully realize that you are sacrificing plenty by not going out, but remember dear that love triumphs through sacrifice. You'll be called upon to make greater sacrifices, honey. Ones that will make you cry, but it's all for a good cause dear. And when this war is over we all will have learned to appreciate life so much more that it will be lived much happier. A worthwhile life is never easy honey. I know how you

dream of things to come. I dream of them also—of being happily married—children—

a house—a couple of dogs etc. It all seems an idle dream in such a time of war as this.

But we are engaged in this struggle in order that such dreams may be brought close to

realization. If we can't change the circumstances which surround our lives, at least we

may master them.

This letter may sound a little screwy to you, but perhaps it's because I'm in one

of my very philosophical moods. Men have been coming into the fort all day to replace

those that left yesterday. Music—bands—drums—applause—sorry faces etc. It

kinda makes you feel funny.

I put in for a leave for the 4th and 5th of March. I don't know if I will get it

but I will know in a few days—then I'll let you know.

To add a footnote to this part of Dad's life—most of his military

service was focused on the Asian Theater and he actually served in Japan

for a period of time. What I find so endearing is that once the war had

ended, Dad held no animosity towards the Japanese. Later he would say

to me, "We should learn to understand the differences and then embrace

them." Not every soldier was willing to say that, but in the long run, it

made my Father the bigger man.

As G. K. Chesterton so wisely stated:

The true soldier fights, not because he hates what is in front of him, but because he loves what is behind him[3].

[3] *Illustrated London News,* Jan. 14, 1911.
www.chesterton.org/quotations/war-and-politics/

Chapter Eleven

Help Your Mother

Tony and Helen were born to be together.

And they didn't let anything get in their way.

Even when they went before the Catholic priest in order to inquire if he would perform their wedding ceremony. Can you envision it? The Italian Catholic seated next to the Scotch Irish Methodist in the priest's dark wooded paneled office. None of the three are sitting comfortably. There is a tension in the room that is palpable. Tony is sweating, Helen nervously tries to conceal her quivering hands and the priest's brow is furrowed so deeply one could plant the spring crop.

The conversation was brief and direct. "I won't be able to marry you," the priest said, his eyes staring directly at my dad.

"Why not?" Dad asked.

The priest looked down at his desk, as if to gather his thoughts, yet the reason was perfectly clear.

"Because Helen is not a Catholic," he stated flatly.

"Oh really?" Dad responded, his face and neck reddening to the degree of a fine ragù.

"That's right," the priest continued. "And Tony, if you marry her, you'll go to Hell."

If this were a cartoon, this would be the moment when the upper portion of Tony's head would magically separate and lift from the rest of his body, as a burst of steam would appear, complete with the sound of a screeching whistle.

Grabbing Mom's hand, the two of them stood up and headed for the door, as Dad made one final turn back towards the priest, shouting, "Well I'm going to marry her---so I'll see *you* in Hell!"

*   *   *

With their marriage beginning under such dramatic circumstances, it is no wonder that when Dad was in the Army, he would enlist my help in taking care of his blessed bride.

Right around the time I was six years old, he wrote me this letter:

Darling Linda,

I hear you'd like to have a little brother? Well, honey,--someday if God is willing, you may have one. Are you sure you would be nice to him? I suppose you would because you are a very thoughtful and unselfish girl. I suppose you had a nice Christmas. It's too bad it rained and you were not able to go to Nani's house and see the other children. Especially Carol Ann. You usually have such nice times with her. By the way—I'd sure like to pinch those new pants you got for Christmas—just to see if I like the material—Ha! Also, for your benefit, I had my teeth ground down so they wouldn't hurt so much when I eat you. I'm sure going to eat you when I come back.

I think the pictures you have been cutting out and coloring for me are wonderful. You are doing very well, honey. Keep it up. I also understand that you are becoming quite a piano player. You practice your lessons very seriously honey. The piano is the one useful musical instrument that a person can learn to play. I'd like very much for you to be good. Perhaps you can even teach mother and I. You teach me how to play the piano and I'll teach you how to sing "Oh, Marie." Ha!

Are you being a nice girl? Mother says you are behaving pretty good. By the time I get home you'll be all grown up and I won't be able to spank you anymore. Ha! I never did anyway, did I? Maybe a little spank once in awhile, but usually we just fooled mother.

You take good care of yourself and be sure Mother and Fluff get plenty of sleep and rest. Make sure you guys eat plenty of that real good spaghetti. It'll make you grow.

I haven't received that card all those school children signed. I suppose I will though. I'll let you know when I do.

Be a nice girl and don't forget to say your prayers every night.

I love you with all of my heart,

Daddy

Later that same year, Dad would write these words to me:

Dear Linda,

I'm very happy to hear you now have a piano. You take your lessons very seriously and I'll bet by the time I come home you will be very good. You must practice every day. You just practice whenever Momie tells you to, and I'm sure you will soon be very good.

I'm glad you are being unselfish about Christmas. I know that piano is a nice gift, but you won't turn something that Santa Claus brings you down—will you?

Honey, now that mother is working, you will have to help her as much as you can. Do whatever she asks you without too much argument. You may not realize it now, but as you grow older you'll find that she is a wonderful Momie. You must help take care of her for me because she's the onliest momie we gots. You make her eat all

her food and get plenty of rest and sleep.

How are you doing in school? I think your writing is wonderful. I'm sorry I

can't come home as you asked in your letter, but be patient darling, by this time next

year we will be together again and have lots of fun.

Goodnight Darling. I love you very much.

Kiss mother for me.

Love

Father

The themes of the two letters overlap. Keep practicing your

piano, eating well, and getting plenty of sleep. And most of all, don't give

your Mother a hard time. Actually, do just the opposite—help her out! I

love how he creates his own phrase--*You must help take care of her for me*

because she's the onliest momie we gots. Taking care of the 'onliest momie.'

How precious is that?

I needed all the encouragement I could get when it came to being

good and helping out. It was easy for me to get sidetracked.

A little too easy.

Most young children enjoy and are fascinated by building tents. The easiest to make were tents made out of bedsheets hung over a clothesline. Having the strict parents that I did, I was never allowed in a tent, surprise, surprise. Dad forbade it. But as a child, I had concluded that the reason I wasn't allowed in a tent was because the air was bad in there. I know, it sounds silly, but that's what I believed.

Well, one day a group of friends finally invited me to enter the tent they had made, which was their clubhouse. I was honored---thrilled to be accepted into this fine club. Once I went in, I was told there was going to be a requirement to join such a fine group of youngsters.

I needed to eat a box of prunes.

I had waited so long for this honor that finally arrived. Needless to say, I followed the request, but never became a member of the club or entered the tent again.

Once again, Dad was right.

Now if only he could get me to obey…

Chapter Twelve
Obey Your Mother

It wasn't enough for me to help take care of Mom. Dad wanted me to obey her, too.

I wasn't a rebellious child, but I did have an independent streak that needed to be dealt with from a parent's perspective.

For example, in my childhood neighborhood was a wonderful stretch of beautiful trees that most people would simply refer to as 'the woods,' but to me it was my 'forest.' Actually, my dad wanted to protect me, so he gave it another name—my 'Forbidden Forest.'

Part of its draw for me was its ample collection of violets. I love violets. I carried a bouquet of violets in my wedding. The temptation to get closer to them was greater than a little girl could resist.

One day I snuck out of the house and headed directly to the 'Forbidden Forest.' My goal was a simple one—"I will pick just one violet and then rush right back out," I convinced myself.

Like bunny rabbits, one quickly became two, two became three and in a forbidden flash, I had a full bouquet of violets—as many as I could clutch in my little hand.

As I ran back home, it suddenly dawned on me that I was going to get in trouble for visiting the 'Forbidden Forest.' I had to concoct a plan that would free me from punishment. I know! I would give the bouquet to my mom.

"Here Mommy, these are for you," I gushed, handing her the violets.

"Thank you, sweetheart," Mom responded, a broad smile enveloping her face.

"That is a lovely bouquet," Dad interjected, and then he went in for the kill. "Where did you get it?"

This was a true dilemma, as I knew I was guilty of entering the "Forbidden Forest,' but now I was faced with the additional pressure of either telling the truth or creating a lie. I went with the truth, hoping my dad would appreciate my obedience to another one of his rules. "I got them in my 'Forbidden Forest'."

Dad's expression grew stern. "Come with me," he said as he led me to my bedroom. "When I say you cannot go to the 'Forbidden Forest', I mean it," he stated matter-of-factly. "You need to learn that when I say 'no,' I mean 'no'."

"Yes, Daddy. I'm sorry, Daddy."

And that was the point when, as we would say back in the 1950's, I 'received his belt.' Ouch.

But I also knew that he was living out the cliché—'this hurts me more than it hurts you.' Learning to obey my parents was a fundamental exercise in our house all throughout my years at home.

*   *   *

Even when Dad was away in the Army, he would instruct me on the importance of my obedience:

Dear Linda,

I had a talk with several pixies today. They told me you have not been doing what Momie tells you to do.

They said you were not eating good and not flushing the toilet—not washing your hands when you go to the toilet—not washing your hands before you eat—not taking a bath when you are supposed to, but rather you just play in the tub. Also they said you don't pay attention to mother the way you should.

Now Linda, I know you think I'm kidding about pixies, because you don't think they are real, but these are Japanese kind and they are real. In fact, I asked one to come home with me when I come home and he said he would, just to keep you company. He's real cute and wears a little blue jacket and little red cap. You'll just love him. Also, he has a little sister who may also come along. She's a little sweetie.

Also Linda, I think you should listen to Mother because she's the only one we gots. We both love her so we should both do as she says to make things easier for her.

Good night darling—I just wish it was next winter also.

God bless you,

Daddy

All throughout my childhood, Dad and Mom taught me the importance of obeying them. Whether it was the lure of blooming violets in the 'Forbidden Forest' or the resistance to eating my vegetables, my parents were on the case when it came to obedience.

A few years later—I must have been 10 or 11, I had another display of disobedience, also framed in the 'Forbidden Forest.' This time I was not in the forest alone. I was with a neighbor. A neighbor boy. An older neighbor boy.

As we wandered through the grove of trees, a slight breeze making the scene even more idyllic, we came upon an ant hill. I was curious, but the neighbor boy held me back with his arm against my stomach. "Don't go any closer," he warned, with a tone in his voice that sounded like the ants were armed and dangerous. Solemnly he turned to me and announced, "Those ants are poisonous."

"What should we do?" I asked, both urgently and innocently.

"There may be ants already on you," he explained. With complete seriousness he said to me, "You need to take down your pants."

I was young, but I wasn't dumb. I took off in a sprint that got me home in record time. Breathlessly, I explained to my parents what had taken place.

Dad went berserk.

He marched out the front door and headed to the house where the older neighbor boy lived. Dad pounded on the door until it was finally answered by the kid's Father.

"Do you know what your son just did?" Dad said in a voice loud enough to be heard back at Pearl Harbor. Before the man could respond, Dad regaled him with a blow by blow of 'Poison Ants in the Forbidden Forest.'

"I don't ever want to see your son around my daughter ever again," Dad insisted. "As a matter of fact, if I ever see him as much as walking by our house, I'll see to it that he never walks again!"

It wasn't the only time Dad had to look out for me.

A few years later, when I was 14 years old, I attended the wedding of an old neighborhood friend's child. This was my first official night out, dressing up and enjoying a first-class band, lovely food and a host of others wearing their very best. I was seated with my parents and a young man came to our table asking me to dance. I had never danced with a boy before, but I loved the music and, after all, I was wearing my best dress, so I said yes. My parents were distracted, talking with some other friends, so they did not realize that I had accepted this dance.

Oh, how I was enjoying my first dance! I was in a trance, envisioning myself as Ginger Rogers and my dancing partner was Fred Astaire.

Without warning, the glorious moment was interrupted by a strong tap, tap, tap on my shoulder. Could this be another suitor cutting in on my first dance? Oh, the ecstasy!

No. It was no suitor. It was Dad. "Linda, go sit down," he ordered me as if I was one of his soldiers back in the Army. I walked back over to our table, but I could hear him giving this young man a piece of his mind.

"Young man, I never want to see you near my daughter," he scolded. Even though my father knew the boy's mother well, it did not keep him from protecting me.

Dad continued, "I know your reputation...you are a bad boy."

I was shocked. This young man was handsome and well dressed. I must say, he was even a good dancer, if only for a few brief steps.

Years later, I would realize that my protective father was right, once again. That young man, sadly, lived up to his poor reputation. I, thankfully, was saved from any future embarrassment.

*   *   *

Through his letters and through his life, Dad was committed to see that I grew up obedient and respectful. It's been said that when it comes to disciplining children, the key to discipline is self-discipline. Dad prided himself in his consistency, as well as the loving standards that he set.

One last thought, just to show he wasn't just a disciplining machine, but a loving, caring parent as well...

...There were numerous times in my formative years when Dad would take me to the bedroom for my punishment, but then only pretend to give me the belt, with me crying out in pain, all to fake out my mother! It was a little secret only Dad and I shared, and we laughed about it together for years.

Gee, it's starting to sound like Dad was never wrong. Perfect. A Superhero. Maybe it's time to set the record straight on that concept.

Chapter Thirteen

He's Only Human!

Since we ended the last chapter with a look at Dad in his true humanity—'pretending' to give me the belt in order to fake out my mother, perhaps this would be a good time to share a few stories to make sure you know that as super human as Dad appears in some of these accounts, the truth is, he was only human.

In the years Dad was home, after his military service, our home was run like a typical home in the 1950's. Mom was very active in the cooking and the cleaning and overall house management, whereas Dad was responsible for watching sports from his Lazy Boy recliner perfectly located in front of the TV. (Lest you think he didn't do anything I must add that he did take out the trash.)

Mom wasn't involved in a great deal of activities outside the home, but there was one night of the week that was sacrosanct. Mom was on a bowling team.

One night, as Mom was getting ready to head down to the bowling alley, she informed Dad and me of an assignment. "I've been working all day on canning some peaches," she began. "They are in mason jars inside the oven right now. Since I need to leave, I need you two to take the jars out of the oven when they're ready and place them on the stove top. That's all I need. Just that one thing. Can you do that for me?"

"Not a problem, honey," Dad assured her, as I nodded in agreement as well.

"Swell," Mom replied cheerfully, giving each of us a peck on the cheek. "I'll see you both after I'm through bowling."

When it came time for us to get the jars of canned peaches out of the oven, a task that had been made to sound so simple, ended up being the stuff of folk legend in the Sturrett house for years to come.

Dad grabbed potholders and began lifting the extremely hot jars out of the oven, placing them on the very cool stovetop. We didn't realize the error of this mistake, and the impending result of such a rapid and drastic change in temperature of the glass jars. Soon we were met with catastrophe.

The jars exploded like bombs in an Air Force training film.

Peaches were everywhere. The sticky liquid surrounding the peaches was now hanging off of lights, pots, pans, dishes and appliances, both major and minor. Our tiny 800-square-foot kitchen would never look the same.

When Mom arrived home, and she was past the initial shock of her kitchen turned into peach cobbler, she simply shook her head, softly repeating, "I gave you one job to do. Just one."

*   *   *

Dad knew the truth in the old phrase: "Confession is good for the soul." Even when he messed up, he owned it and tried to make sure it wouldn't happen again.

The following letter has always been a favorite of mine because it illustrates that very point—the value of confession. When one considers that Dad was miles away from Mom at the time of this writing, so that he could have kept this little adventure to himself, it is even more powerful in its transparency.

Dear Helen,

I'm writing this during 10 minute breaks on the machine gun range. As I told you over the phone, I have a pretty full week and I wouldn't be able to write unless I did it this way.

I'm very belligerent today and my morale is very low. Last night we had a problem during which it rained several hours. Everyone naturally got very wet. Well this morning the Captain insisted that the men wear the same uniform. They were so wet and muddy that I objected immediately. They wouldn't listen to me, so I went back to my room and put my wet and muddy clothes on. If my men have to wear them I will too. Some of these high ranking officers around here have no concern about the men, and it sure makes me angry. I'd sure like to fight some of them, but they'd only court martial me if I did.

It was soothing to hear your voice last night. Kind of makes me miss you. I was so tired and disgusted last Saturday that I decided to do something I'd never done before "Get drunk." Wow! I'm still trying to find out what happened. I went into a cocktail lounge in Washington and ordered a drink. I don't remember how many I had, or where I went from there, but I woke up in a dancing studio. I don't remember going there, but the two girls who own it said they adopted me the night before at a party at an apartment somewhere in Baltimore (50 miles away). They said I was having a lot of fun and apparently had lost whoever I'd come there with, so they took me home with them. They said I wasn't too drunk, but they were afraid I'd get lost in my condition.

I'd never been drunk before, and I don't know when I will ever do that again, because I had a terrific hangover and spent most of my spare time the next day between classes with an ice bag on my head (Ha!).

I've been doing a lot of thinking about you lately, honey. I can't wait till I get a chance to come home again. Perhaps it's just because I miss my mother (Ha!). Anyway, I expect to be home sometime in August but I'm not sure yet, just when during the month. I'll let you know. Meantime, keep writing me lots of letters. You know I love to receive them.

I'll write again just as soon as I can. Tomorrow I'm taking my men through a field where they will be firing real machine guns at us. Oh boy!

Coo Coo

My love

*　　*　　*

Let's review, shall we?

To my dear Sweetheart:

1. I'm blue.

2. I decided to go out and get drunk.

3. I got so drunk I didn't even know what was going on.

4. The next thing I knew I was in the company of two girls.

5. Apparently, I spent the night with them.

6. I am now back on the base, but with a horrible hangover.

Your loving

boyfriend.

That is so much like my dad. I messed up, but I have to get it off my chest. And he wasted no time. As he mentioned in the beginning of the letter, he was writing it during ten-minute breaks on the machine gun range. He didn't want there to be any excess time between the sin and the confession.

What you don't know is that when I look at my collection of letters from my father, most all of them are written on standard issue government stationery, either 6 by 9 inches or 5 by 8 inches. There is one letter that stands out as the exception—this confession of my father's wild night in Baltimore. It's written on paper that measures just 3 by 5 inches. To say everything he wanted to say, there are no less than eight of these small slips of paper, which I guess was easier to tuck away in a pocket while shooting his machine gun!

There's an old Chinese proverb that states:

A clear conscience is the greatest armor.

Let's just say that, like a good knight, my dad was always well protected and well prepared.

Chapter Fourteen

The Power of 'Ha!'

My dad knew the value of a good sense of humor.

We see it woven into the fabric of most all of his letters that he sent home. Dad's signature word was 'Ha!' It extended beyond his writings to the way he lived his life.

Think about some of the sentences we've read from his letters:

I'm still as rough as ever, and I'd probably be pushing your nose—biting or twisting your arm around a bedpost—or even smashing your finger in a nutcracker if you were here right now. Ha!

Dad could move from the most tender of thoughts to the real-life awkwardness of bites, twists and smashes. Just looking at those words again makes me smile.

Another example was in his classic double postscript:

P.S. I'll even take Linda for a walk once in awhile.

P.S: When she learns how to change her own diaper. Ha!

Gee, I love you Momie

Dad would willingly offer his help to Mom in taking care of me, but he humorously drew the line at changing diapers. He seemed to have lots of fun with the whole idea of not only being a husband, but a new father as well.

He wrote it this way:

I'm well aware that there are two women in my life now, but neither of them are going to be nagging because I will take immediate action to prevent such a thing. First, I will make you stand in the corner and next I will put a gag around Linda's mouth. Ha! I'll show you both who's boss.

The picture is clear: No nagging—understand? If there is nagging, Mom will be sent to the corner while I am gagged. Dad is humorously and vividly showing us who will be the boss!

And how about his classic methods of building up the morale of his men?

I've done everything I could to bring their morale up. I got right down in the mud with them and ruined a $40 trench coat and an $18 pair of pants. I bought them

$25 worth of hot dogs, $10 worth of candy bars. I sang songs for them. I've told jokes to make them laugh and now it's up to them. I've got 'em so they'd rather qualify on the range today than get a 30 day furlough. They're trying hard because they don't want to let me down.

"I've told them jokes to make them laugh," he writes. Oh, how I wish there was a video of my dad leading his men. I envision guts, determination, and some good hard belly laughs.

Dad's favorite word "Ha!" even found its way into more serious subjects:

He said, "You know so much about the construction you speak about that it doesn't seem possible that you are not really an engineer." Ha! What he doesn't know is that I spend hours studying the blue prints and specifications before I talk to anyone about any job.

"Ha! What he doesn't know…" I see my dad smiling down on his paper and pen as he recounts this significant moment to my mom.

I had a talk with several pixies today. They told me you have not been doing what Momie tells you to do.

Can you imagine my mom reading this letter to me? Dad developed the idea of 'pixies' to the point that there was one dressed in blue who had a sister dressed in red. Talk about a fun imagination! As Mom and I smiled through its reading, the letter made its point, and I obeyed my mom better.

I was so tired and disgusted last Saturday that I decided to do something I'd never done before "Get drunk." Wow! I'm still trying to find out what happened.

There's not a lot that needs to be said about this letter. Dad's one and only drunken night is hilarious.

I've been doing a lot of thinking about you lately, honey. I can't wait till I get a chance to come home again. Perhaps it's just because I miss my mother (Ha!).

People who study humor tell us that an effective way to make people laugh is by setting them up one way and then surprising by going another way. (Often called 'the punch line'). Here, Dad looks like he's going to say he misses my mom, but he shifts and says he misses *his mom.* He's kidding, of course, but the humor works. Here's another version that is my favorite:

126

I miss you—just a little—or maybe a little more than just a little—and I'm looking forward to holding you in my arms. I'm sure lucky to have a gal like you. You're such a sweet—honest—homely little farmerette. (Ha!) Fooled ya.

No kidding darling—I do miss you quite a bit. Fought off a strong urge to call you last night.

> *Love,*
>
> *Michael, your sweetheart*
>
> *HA!*

This one is a veritable cornucopia of laughter. It's all about the unexpected. I'm sure Mom was expecting words of love, complimenting her beauty, and maybe even signed with a mushy nickname.

What does she get instead? She is called 'homely.' She is called a 'farmerette.' And, my personal favorite, he signs off with 'Michael, your sweetheart.' You'll have to agree with me, my mom must've been smiling from ear to ear when she read the comedy stylings of her guy.

Love and laughter just go together.

*   *   *

No one appreciated my dad's sense of humor more than my husband, Bob. You've probably figured out by now that DeHoff is not an Italian name. Bob's family is Dutch. Despite the differences in their backgrounds and upbringing, my dad was good to Bob—but not above having some fun with him.

The circumstances of their first encounter still make me smile. In a totally uncharacteristic manner, Dad liked Bob from the start. None of my other suitors ever had that advantage. Bob was already working hard at a career in real estate. Dad found that quite impressive. After the two men first met, Dad found a moment to take me aside and give me an immediate impression.

With a smile a mile wide, Dad announced, "I like this guy!" And after the appropriate pause he added, "He tried to sell me some land!"

(As an aside, Bob won my mother over very quickly as well. My earliest memories of the two of them find Mom in the kitchen cooking up home fries. Bob is right next to her, watching every move. As she takes each slice of potato out of the frying pan, Bob is right there, gobbling up each one of them. Mom couldn't have been happier.)

My Dutch husband got the thrill of his life when the Sturrett extended family put him through an initiation process that cemented his status in our family:

My Aunt Angie's husband was known to all of us as Uncle T. He owned and operated a concrete company and was an avid cook and gardener. He grew the most beautiful peace roses and vegetables one could imagine. But perhaps he was most proud of his sausage recipe.

Everyone raved over his delicious sausage and constantly urged Uncle T to make it commercially. But Uncle T wouldn't hear of it. To this day it remains the best sausage I have ever tasted.

His olive relish recipe was equally as delicious and famous as his sausage. Family and friends begged for his deeply secretive olive relish recipe, but to no avail. Uncle T refused to share it with anyone. One blistery, snowy winter evening, around roughly 9:30, Uncle T called our house, and with a broken Italian accent, said, "I needa talk to Roberto now."

"Of course, Uncle T, I'll get him," I answered and handed Bob the receiver. He listened for less than a minute before immediately hanging up the phone and beginning to dress. "What did Uncle T say?" I asked.

"Your uncle said he's making the olives. That's all he said. Don't wait up for me," was all Bob would say.

Bob arrived, at around 10:30 and was immediately taken to the basement where Uncle T had all the raw ingredients scattered on a big table with a large bottle of his homemade wine and two glasses, one for him and one for Bob, filled to the brim. In retelling the story later, Bob

adds, "I thought I was going to see Jimmy Hoffa walk around the corner!"
Needless to say, Bob returned home very late that night.

But the rest is Sturrett family history. It was on that occasion that
Uncle T shared his famous olive relish recipe with Bob only. At that
moment, Bob was now officially a member of our family...a true passage.

The following Sunday at dinner my dad announced, "You are now
an Honorary Italian!", patting Bob on the back. By the way, Bob has kept
Uncle T's secret and who knows, may someday share it with others.

The urgent visit to Uncle T's would be played out one more time
in the life of Tony and Bob. But in the next chapter, it was just the two of
them.

Chapter Fifteen

History, the Guest and Three Cakes

January 17, 1970.

A Saturday.

A crisp, clear day. The weatherman predicted it would get all the way up to 39 degrees, with no rain or snow in the Canton forecast.

It was the day Dad and Mom had prepared me for in the 25 years I was under their care.

It was my wedding day.

It was also a day that history was made at Saint Michael the Archangel Catholic Church. Let me explain. The Sturrett family is best described as 'Italian, Catholic, and Democrat.' Whereas the DeHoff family is best described as 'German, Protestant, and Republican.' When the Lord's Prayer was said by all in attendance, it was the groom's side of the church that recited the Lord's Prayer with passionate enthusiasm! Whereupon the young priest officiating our wedding, Father O'Neil, paused and said, "Tonight, history has been made. I think the Protestants outnumbered the Catholics!"

One of the more unusual facts about our wedding day is that the date—January 17th—was not just our wedding day, it was also my dad's birthday, as well as the birthday of our officiating priest. We knew we couldn't let special days like that go unnoticed, so we made arrangements for a proper celebration...

...we had *three* cakes at our reception!

The more I've had the time to think about that circumstance, I have decided that there was even more symbolism than originally intended. Three is an important number. And when it comes to marriage, there's an old adage that goes something like this: It takes three to create a successful marriage; a man, a woman, and God.

And we had a cake for each one of us.

That's how Dad ended his Magnum Opus letter to me. Remember?

*Your husband, your family, your home—**your entire life can be truly valuable only if you have a guest in your house and that guest is <u>God.</u>** There's been too much happiness in our home, Linda, for me to believe that your mother and I have created it all by ourselves. I think we've had some outside help. And if our happiness is a reward from God for the way we've lived, then I want you to go on as we* *are living, because you deserve the same happiness in your own home that you'll start*

someday.

Dad's faith in God was unwavering. It had been that way from the start. As a young boy, Dad attended Saint Anthony Catholic Church, which is the historic Italian neighborhood parish.

When he said that happiness was God's reward for the way we've lived, he meant it. He lived his life in an upright manner. People respected him, and that was due to his high moral standards.

There were plenty of Sundays when Dad chose the golf course over the church sanctuary, but his connection to the spiritual world was unquestionable. Before he went off to war, his mom gave him a medal of the Holy Mother to wear. As he left for his military service, his mother pointed to the medal and said to him, "You're going to be okay."

And he was.

To carry this story out further, years later, when it was time for me to go off to college, Dad gave me that medal of the Holy Mother to wear. I was so impressed with how thoughtful it was for him to do that.

However, while I was at college, the unthinkable occurred.

I lost the medal.

Panic stricken; I did the only thing I could think of. The only thing that Dad would do at a time like that.

I prayed and prayed and prayed.

And believe it or not, by the next morning, my prayers had been answered.

What do I mean by that?

When I awoke the next morning, the medal of the Holy Mother was on my shoulder.

I have no other explanation other than God performed a miracle.

*   *   *

Dad faithfully believed in Scripture teachings on the subject of family. One of the finest biblical passages in the Bible on God's place as the foundation of our families is found in the Old Testament book of the Psalms. Look at God's Words from Psalm 127:

Psalm 127

Unless the Lord builds the house,
They labor in vain who build it;
Unless the Lord guards the city,
The watchman keeps awake in vain.

² It is vain for you to rise up early,

To retire late,

To eat the bread of painful labors;

For He gives to His beloved even in his sleep.

³ Behold, children are a gift of the Lord,

The fruit of the womb is a reward.

⁴ Like arrows in the hand of a warrior,

So are the children of one's youth.

⁵ How blessed is the man whose quiver is full of them;

They will not be ashamed

When they speak with their enemies in the gate.

There are a lot of good lessons contained in those five verses. It's God who is building our wonderful home, not human effort. One can do a great deal of the work, but it is the Lord Himself who chooses to bless our home.

Children are God's gift. Children are rewards. Parents who have been blessed by God should do their very best to impart wisdom, teach good morals, and provide unending amounts of love, support and comfort to their children.

Simple to say, but Dad was one of those rare guys who actually chose to live out Psalm 127 during his life. He was the human embodiment of this psalm and treated me as his most priceless and precious of gifts.

* * *

Dad made sure I said my prayers every night. When he was home, he would join me, together on our knees at my bedside. When he was away, he would write and remind me to do it.

Hi Ya honey,

I sure miss you sitting on my lap and pestering me for 6 cents for a popsicle. I also miss your being hungry every night before you go to bed and **I also miss saying your prayers with you.** *I guess I just miss you. I'm going to bring you something but I really don't know what. However, don't be too disappointed if I don't because I may not have a chance.*

See you Friday.

Love

Daddy

I also love how Dad sneaks a little reminder into this letter about going to church together:

Dear Linda,

How are you? Mother tells me in her letters that you are being a very good girl while she's working. I understand, also, that you go right to sleep in the evenings when mother tells you to. That's swell, Lin. I'm proud of you. I've shown your's and mother's picture to all the guys around here and they think you are both beautiful, but

you don't look at all like me. Of course, I told them your feet look like mine anyway.
Ha!

I'm glad you are going to Catechism with mother. When I come home we can all go to church together. Won't that be fun? You and I have never been in church together, have we?

I bought Mother a lovely candy dish to put your candy in. I also bought you a silver charm bracelet with little silver things hanging on it. You can sure show off in school with it. Now don't you be afraid to go see Santa Claus at school. You know— you don't know who the man is, but I'll bet it's Mickie's daddy. You keep on being a nice girl, Lin. When I get home we are sure going to have some nice times together. I might even play cards with you. Ha! I love you very much and miss you.

All my love,

Daddy

P.S. X x x

Simple commands. Say your prayers. Go to church. But don't be misled by the simplicity. It's the bits and pieces from which solid homes are built.

*   *   *

Dad lived to be 87 years old. During some of the final years of his life, he suffered from lung disease. It was discovered that one of his lungs had a benign tumor on it, yet the tumor had to be removed.

In one of his hospitalizations at the end of his life, he was required to take a daily test, constituting of blowing into a tube as hard as he could for as long as he could. Of all the piercing and prodding done by the medical staff, it was that darn tube test that Dad hated the most.

So, one day, as the nurse entered his room with the tube in her hands, Dad motioned her over close to him and was overheard whispering in her ear: *"Honey, if you don't make me blow into that tube, I promise, I'll leave you something in my will!"*

The nurse smiled sweetly but placed the tube in Dad's mouth anyway.

I'm not sure the nurse knew it, but truth be told, Dad didn't even have a will.

Dad had one other heartfelt conversation in his later years. My husband Bob and I were at home one day when the phone rang. It was Dad. "Hi Dad!" I answered cheerily.

"Put Bob on the phone," Dad instructed, without any acknowledgement of his favorite daughter on the line.

I handed the phone to Bob. "Hi Dad," Bob said.

"Bob, I want you to come quickly over to my house," Dad said, with an air of secrecy and urgency in his voice. "I have a personal matter to discuss with you."

"Sure, Dad, I'm on my way," Bob replied and then he jumped into our car.

Bob was sure something was wrong. On the drive over, he was preparing himself for the worst—like maybe Dad had some terrible disease and wouldn't have very much longer to live. Bob knew that Dad was a man of strategy, so perhaps he was going to let Bob in on some secret plan for his last days. Maybe it even involved a little money buried in the back yard!

Once at Dad's house, Bob was invited in and taken immediately to the room farthest away from the front door. Closing the study door behind him, Dad invited Bob to sit down. "Come close to me. I want to tell you something and I don't want anyone else to hear."

"Okay, Dad," Bob answered, moving as close to Dad as he could.

In a voice just above a whisper, Dad said to Bob, "Be certain you tell no one, okay?" Dad nodded silently.

And with that, Dad uttered the news that was so urgent. *"I think I am becoming a Regan Republican."* (Keep in mind, Dad was a lifelong Democrat.)

I think Dad must have died with a smile on his face.

He loved God, so he wasn't afraid to die.

And he loved to laugh, so he brought joy to all he met.

And he had lived his life well, so his mission on earth was accomplished.

Epilogue

A Letter to Dad

Dear Dad,

It's been a long time since you went to Heaven in 2004, and I'm guessing you already know how much I miss you. But revisiting the lovely letters that you wrote Mom and me have kept you in the forefront of my life in a most powerful way.

For a guy who didn't speak English until he entered the second grade, you did really good for yourself! Dad, thank you for all that you added to my life. Not the least of which was that beautiful letter you wrote me when I was only six. God was gracious—He brought you home from war safely, so when I opened that letter as a teenager, you were right there with me. I have done my best to apply the advice that you gave me, and I'm hoping you agree that a marriage of over fifty years proves that what you wrote me must really work!

It's springtime in Canton right now and I find myself traveling back in time, imagining you are still here, thinking about what it might look like if I were able to create for you 'the perfect day.' In my mind, I'm a little girl still living at home and we're all together on a wonderful weekend. It's partly cloudy, but the temperature is a perfect 72 degrees. It's Saturday afternoon, so that means you've already knocked out eighteen holes with your buddies at your favorite golf course. Back in the clubhouse, you regaled the boys with some of your favorite stories over a sandwich, a cup of coffee and a game of pinochle.

You look great, by the way. You always did. I remember you telling me that as a young man, you were always impeccably dressed for your dates. Then you would smile and tell me why you always looked so well put together. You would talk your sister Angie into ironing your shirts. She would agree but only after charging you 5 cents per shirt. "Sometimes I would owe her as much as 25 cents but my shirts always looked great!" you would tell me with a wink and a grin. You always looked so dapper.

Now you're home from golf, and you're comfortably seated in your recliner, catching an afternoon Cleveland Indians baseball game on TV. The Detroit Tigers are in town for a three-game series. The Indians won last night, so as usual, you are hoping for a sweep by the Tribe. In between innings, however, you switch the channel to watch the golf tournament. Since it's only Saturday, you know you'll watch every hole again tomorrow, since Sunday is the day the winner is determined. But today you're hoping the cameras will catch a powerful drive or a miraculous putt by the Golden Bear, Jack Nicklaus. And they need to catch that shot while the baseball game is airing a commercial.

On your lap is today's edition of The Cleveland Plain Dealer, *opened, of course, to the sports page. There's a feature article on a new player the Browns picked up in an off-season trade, but you just shake your head as you read, muttering, "They're just not the same since Paul Brown left."*

In a scenario that can only be described as 'the perfect day,' not only did you win your early morning golf match, but the Indians topped the Tigers with a walk off home run, and Jack Nicklaus is on top of the leaderboard going into tomorrow's finals of the televised golf tournament. And just like you had hoped, you got to see him hit his finest shot of the day. Is there anything else that could make this day more perfect?

Yes.

A great Italian meal.

Mom has outdone herself as the three of us sit around the dinner table, enjoying a 'Sicilian splendor.' As it was on most nights, Dad, you are in charge of the topics of conversation, so Mom and I listen with interest as you weave together tales of some of your favorite characters: Your parents, of course. And don't forget Franklin Delano Roosevelt. Or your sports idols. It's all very pleasant, until you bring up a recent decision made by the U.S. Supreme Court. You're not in agreement with them and you stand by your customary summary: "Lin, their job is to interpret the laws, not make them."

Mom doesn't like to see you getting upset so she asks you to change the subject. As you begin, you wink at me and say, "Did I ever tell you the story about being the number one salesman at a woman's shoe store?" He has told us that story before and he knows that Mom doesn't care for it, so the joke is made and the conversation moves on to other issues, such as when your oldest brother, Carl, was a salesman at Sears, or a new magazine article that you read at the barber shop about Ike Eisenhower.

I must say, you always saw to it that our conversations were entertaining, but they were also deep. We debated hot topics. We role-played. We resisted the superficial and got down deep in the weeds. Lest you ever got accused of being boring, you peppered your stories with a generous dose of humor. Just as you added to your letters, that wonderful word—"Ha!"

After dinner, maybe your 'perfect day' will include an episode of the Saturday Night Fights featuring a couple of your favorite boxers. Mom's bountiful Italian meal may make you a little drowsy on the recliner, but that's part of the perfection now, isn't it? Go ahead and fall asleep. We can get the outcome of the fight in tomorrow's sports page.

Your 'perfect day' can conclude with you sleeping peacefully, knowing your approach to life has been set forth for more to see and hopefully has encouraged many to move their lives in a better direction.

I love you Dad,

Linda

Afterword

A Call to Action

Dear Precious Reader,

It is my hope that by sharing these letters with you, I have inspired you to write a letter of your own. Share your hopes and your dreams with your child, a loved one, or a good friend. It is not about perfect grammar or punctuation, but rather about sharing heartfelt and mindful thoughts with someone that you love!

Your words could very well make all the difference in their life. Therefore, it could change a family, a neighborhood, and a community. History has shown that it could even change the world. I know the letters I received from my father have certainly changed my life.

Maybe it's the day your child is born, their first day of school, their graduation day, their first day of college or a new job, to mark an engagement or on their wedding day – whatever, the occasion or milestone, take the time to write a handwritten letter. We have today, we may not have tomorrow!

It's never too late. If ever there was a time in our lives, given the current social unrest and political turmoil in our country and the world, now is the time for each of us to express our love, our thoughts, our wisdom, our hopes, and our dreams to those that we cherish, young or old, family or friends, and born or unborn. It can make all the difference in a person's life. It already has. Let's start today.

Today is a great day to inspire great change,

Linda DeHoff

Pictured: Tony, my father.